# STENCILING

# STENCILING

### A THOROUGH MODERN GUIDE TO THE ENJOYABLE
### ❧ & ELEGANT ART WHERE BEGINNER & EXPERT ARE ONE ❧

**by Pamela Riddle & Mary Jane Danley**

**photographs by Julio Rodriguez**
**illustrations by Mary Jane Danley**

A BERKLEY WINDHOVER BOOK
published by
BERKLEY PUBLISHING CORPORATION

Berkley Publishing Corporation
200 Madison Avenue
New York, N.Y. 10016

SBN 425-03822-X

*BERKLEY WINDHOVER BOOKS are published by
Berkley Publishing Corporation
200 Madison Avenue
New York, N.Y. 10016*

Berkley Windhover Book ® TM 1062206

Printed in the United States of America

Berkley Windhover Edition, OCTOBER, 1978

Designed by Virginia M. Smith

*For John E. Danley,*
*with sincere appreciation and love*
*from his wife,*
*and*
*For Pamela's new baby Amanda,*
*for the luck she will bring.*

# Contents

# Introduction

It is difficult to pinpoint an exact time or place when and where stenciling began, but historical opinion is that the craft began before recorded history in the Middle East and the Orient. The first stencils were probably leaves, twigs, or petals laid down to create patterns on cloth. The invention of actual stencils themselves has been attributed to both the Chinese and Egyptians between 2000 and 3000 B.C. The earliest verifiable stenciling is said to have been discovered in caves in Western China by an Englishman, Sir Aurel Stein, in the early part of the twentieth century. The pieces that Stein found date back to about 1000 A.D. The Japanese, however, contributed their unique grace to the stenciling with delicate designs that date back to the sixth century A.D.

Trade routes between China and the Middle East were probably responsible for the mingling of the art styles. Trade routes were also noted for carrying the art to Western Europe where some stenciled work began to appear during the Middle Ages in both France and Switzerland. In reference to their origin, these intricate shapes cut from very thin strips of wood were known as arabesques.

In some cases, the arabesques were applied directly to a piece of furniture in an effort to simulate inlaid work. This was most often the case among the more affluent cityfolk. Country people would paint through the arabesque and use it again and again to decorate their more modest surroundings. Much of this early stencil work, done in country churches to decorate pews and choir stalls, can still be seen in rural French and Swiss churches.

Stencils also began to become popular with printers who used them to color in woodcuts. Soon they achieved one of their most popular uses as the French, particularly, began using stencils to create beautiful wallpapers. Other Europeans quickly followed suit. Another extremely popular item by the fifteenth and sixteenth centuries were decks of elaborately stenciled playing cards.

By the seventeenth century, books of stencil patterns began to appear which people could browse through and adapt to their own needs and homes.

In the American colonies stenciling was a simple and cheap method of decorating the primitive rough-hewn wood and plaster of the earliest dwellings. Settlers with more money often sent to Europe for more sophisticated stenciled items like furniture and floorcloths (a forerunner of linoleum made of an oilcloth that was stenciled and then stretched tightly across a floor). Stenciling wooden floors in patterns that attempted to imitate woven rugs was also popular. Often the floor patterns or details from them would be reproduced on walls, moldings, and fireplace mantels as well.

Although people could create and paint their own designs, stenciling became a respected occupation. Traveling stencil artists would go from place to place, remaining with a household until all of the work that had been contracted for was completed. Most of these traveling artists remain unknown, but the work of at least one of them—Moses Eaton—became so recognizable and desirable that he, his brothers, sons and their unique designs remain famous today.

Well-known manufacturers like Lambert Hitchcock (whose unique furniture still bears his name) and clockmaker Seth Thomas were among those who used stencils on their products. Hitchcock, incidentally, was one of the first large-scale employers of women. He found that they were more patient and exacting and far more capable than men at producing the intricate designs.

No discussion of the history of stenciling would be complete without a nod to Louis Comfort Tiffany whose beautiful and still much sought-after glasswork followed stencil patterns.

With the exception of Tiffany's work, stenciling began to wane by the mid-nineteenth century. The Victorians used a bit of stenciled fabric with their velvet work, but otherwise the craft became virtually dormant. Mass production and new styles left it dated. Yet, it has continued to have popular revivals.

The current resurgence of interest goes hand-in-hand with the desire that people have to express their own unique personality in all areas of life, from the way they dress to the way they decorate their homes. Crafts like stenciling allow for that individuality. It allows you to put your own signature on a wall, a floor, a mirror, a shirt.

Part of the appeal of stenciling is that one need not be Michelangelo to create great beauty. The process is simple and most people become adept quickly. Another facet of its appeal is its versatility since stenciling can be applied to almost any surface and the range of designs are limited only by imagination.

In the next chapters the materials and methods of stenciling will be discussed. Ideas for choosing designs and directions for adapting them for stenciling will be given. There is also an invaluable Design Portfolio of stencils created especially for this book.

Read on and become acquainted with this delightful, simple, and inexpensive, but richly rewarding craft. We have found that the hardest thing about stenciling is to learn self-control. Once you see what beautiful things you can create, you won't want to stop. It is tremendously addicting. Plain walls and floors, curtains, and sheets seem to beckon and you won't be able to pass an antique store or yard sale without stopping to look for something to decorate. Unchecked, you can get completely out of hand and overstencil your wardrobe and household. Just learn to curb yourself. Besides, once you do your home and clothing, people will be clamoring for gifts of your work. You can then channel your energy into gift-giving or—who knows?—you might even have found a new source of income!

# CHAPTER ONE

# Materials

STENCILING IS A decorative process where color is applied to a surface through a design cut out of a nonabsorbent material. Many people only regard it as a dated craft, suitable only to period furniture and tinware. Nothing is further from the truth. The process can very easily be applied to decorate and enhance almost anything from a T-shirt to a brick wall. All you need to consider are the properties of the surface to be stenciled and suitable choices of stenciling material and coloring agent.

Only a few tools are needed for stenciling— tools that are relatively simple to acquire and use. Even better, they are inexpensive. Stenciling is not a craft that requires you to break the bank before you even begin. Basically, you will need material from which to cut stencils, tools to cut with, colors to apply, and something to apply them with. In addition there are some simple odds and ends usually found right at home that are useful to have handy when stenciling. We will discuss the general items here. If any stenciling, such as on food, requires special materials, they are discussed and described within the specific chapters.

*Shown here is an assortment of materials that might be used in a stencil project. It is always a good idea to gather your materials ahead of time and arrange them on a tray. Everything you will need is within easy reach and you won't have to stop work because you have forgotten tape, or a pencil, or the brushes you need.*

## Stenciling Material

There is a large variety of materials to use for cutting stencils and probably each of them will serve as well on nearly any surface. Some are better than others for various reasons.

*Acetate* in flat sheets with a gauge of .0075 is our unqualified favorite. We specify flat sheets because although it does come in rolls, no amount of gymnastics seems to be enough to flatten it out to the point that makes cutting a stencil easy. In flat sheets, however, acetate is wonderful. It is easy to cut and it is transparent which also makes cutting easier. Another advantage of transparency is that many sheets of acetate may be superimposed on one another, which facilitates cutting successive stencils for one design. Acetate is also easily cleaned if it gets too smeared with paint. Last, it is extremely durable. You will be able to use a design cut from acetate over and over again.

The flat sheets we mentioned are sold individually and also come in a tablet form with twenty or twenty-five sheets per pad. If .0075 gauge acetate is not available, you can substitute .0050 gauge. It has all of the properties of .0075 gauge, except that it is thinner. This makes it tear more easily, so a little extra care must be taken if you use it.

*Mylar and vinyl* are similar to acetate and may be used as stencil material as well, although acetate is superior to either of them. Mylar is not as transparent as acetate and therefore only three or four sheets can be superimposed conveniently. This can limit the amount of detail you can produce with a single design. Vinyl is transparent, but it is not as rigid as acetate or mylar. It can wrinkle as you work with it and cause distortion in transferring the design.

*Stencil paper* is usually light brown or off-white in color. It is actually a kind of waxed paper that is semitransparent. It is fairly easy to cut, if somewhat fragile. The waxed surface can also rub onto your cutting blade and prevent your getting nice, sharp, clean edges. Stencil paper is nonabsorbent and relatively inexpensive. It, no doubt, served the purpose before acetate and mylar appeared. But with these other materials available, stencil paper is just not as good. Its lack of transparency adds an extra step in transferring designs. It is not durable; it rips and tears easily

and cannot be used more than a couple of times before a new stencil must be cut. Stencil paper is sold in sheets of 18 inch by 24 inch. If you plan to use it, ask for a .0050 thickness.

*Oak tag and manila paper* can also be used for cutting stencils. Their main asset is that they are cheap. They are good if you are planning to stencil with marking pens, colored pencils, or crayons because they are absorbent materials and will not resist liquid paints. To make them nonabsorbent, you can coat stencils cut from oak tag or manila with shellac. Another drawback of these materials is that they are not transparent, so that any design you use must be transferred directly onto it and this involves an extra step. However, despite its drawbacks, we do find that oak tag and manila paper are just about as good, if not better, than "official" stencil paper. They are cheaper and readily available at any stationery store.

*Plain brown wrapping paper* can also be used for stencils provided that you give it several coats of shellac to strengthen it. Its properties are the same as oak tag or manila paper, but it is even cheaper than either of them.

*Soft woods* in very thin sheets are another suitable material for cutting stencils. Such wooden stencils would be similar to the arabesques mentioned in the Introduction. The design is cut from wood with jigsaws, coping saws, drills, or chisels. The edges of the design have to be beveled so that the underside is larger. Naturally, such stencils have a special use and you would not use them for ordinary painted work. These are used to create three-dimensional relief designs. The openings are filled with a paste made of white glue and water (two parts glue to one part water) and plaster. These are mixed to a stiff consistency and forced through the stencil. The surface is then smoothed with a trowel or putty knife before the stencil is removed. When dry, the relief stencil can be painted as desired.

*Vellum* is another kind of transparent paper available at art and hobby shops. Its qualities are similar to stencil paper. It is nonabsorbent and relatively inexpensive. It is particularly good if you use it on cloth, but it cannot meet the excellence of acetate.

*Zinc or brass* in very thin sheets are used by some craftspeople in cutting stencils. We are not recommending them here for general use, but are mentioning them to make you aware of the wide variety of materials that can be used. Designs must be sketched directly onto the metal and then cut out with drills, files, and other standard metal-cutting tools. If you wish to go through with cutting them out, you will have a stencil that will definitely outlive you, your children, and your children's children.

## Marking and Cutting Tools

*Soft lead pencils* are all that you will need for marking stencil paper, oak tag, manila, and vellum.

*Fine-pointed ballpoint pens or Rapidograph drawing pens* are necessary for marking on acetate, vinyl, or mylar. They are both fine, but the latter represents a substantial (approximately $15.00) investment of cash. You may eventually wish to make the purchase, but for starting out an inexpensive ballpoint (we like Bic best) is all you really need.

*Scissors* will be needed to cut paper or acetate to size. For the various papers, any household pair will do, but for cutting acetate, vinyl, or mylar, we prefer to use a pair of Fiskars Normark scissors. Their shape allows for the best visibility, an important feature since marks tend to mysteriously appear and disappear when you look at acetate for long periods.

*The Grifhold No. 113* swivel knife with a replacement blade of No. 113-B is what we find to be the best all-around, all-purpose cutting tool. It is versatile—cutting large designs and tiny details with equal ease. The blades are durable and capable of cutting as many as fifty designs clearly and cleanly. The Grifhold No. 113 is a very comfortable knife to use. The importance of comfort cannot be stressed enough. Cutting out stencils, especially of large designs with many repeats—or even small ones if you are a beginner—takes its toll on your wrists and hands. If a knife is comfortable to hold and easy to use, it is a tremendous plus. The Grifhold is the star performer as far as we are concerned.

*X-acto knives and Stanley cutting tools* are also good for cutting designs and many craftspeople swear by them. We find, however, that although they are fairly comfortable as far as handling, the blades wear out very quickly and must be changed often. This makes them more expensive to use in the long run than our favorite Grifhold.

*Hole-punchers* are useful for cutting a design where small, uniform circles are a must. They are also good for polka dots, freckles, speckles, and small berries. They are, however, by no means necessary, and you needn't purchase one to begin stenciling.

## Colors

Special coloring materials for various mediums will be discussed in the appropriate chapters later on. Here, we will confine the discussion to the most commonly used and versatile coloring agents.

*Acrylic paints* are the single most versatile paints you can use for stenciling. They are easy to work with and can be used directly from the tube without thinning or thickening. They can be used to tint waterbased background paints and acrylic gesso. Also, these wonderful paints dry quickly—an important factor in stenciling, especially if your design contains more than one color. Acrylics come in a huge assortment of colors which can save you the time of mixing and blending in many cases. They are very easy to clean up, which is always nice. You will also find that acrylics will adhere to almost any surface including wood, ceramics, cloth, leather, metal, paper, and plastic. We cannot recommend these paints highly enough. There are many brands available, but our favorite is Grumbacher's Hyplar Acrylic Polymer paints.

*Japan paints* are also popular with many stencilers. Although we have become enamored with the working ease provided by acrylic paints, we would be seriously remiss in not also recommending that you try japan paints. These are not to be confused with the tubes of enamel paint—also called japan paint—used primarily for tole painting or model painting. To be sure of what you are getting ask for signwriters' japan paints or japan colors. You will find that the colors are flat and opaque and produce beautiful, subtle hues and shadings. Where acrylics can be applied directly from the tube, japan colors must be worked with turpentine to achieve the proper consistency. A little paint will go quite a long way and it dries almost instantly.

*Oil paints* can generally be used wherever you would use acrylics. However, they take an enormously long time to dry—up to a week or more if the weather is damp—and are not practical if the design you are planning to stencil will consist of more than one color. A stencil must stay put until the painted area is dry. Working with several colors of oil paint, could result in a design that will take a few weeks to complete.

*Latex paints* in flat, low-luster, satin, and high-gloss finishes are suitable for stenciling, both as background color and in the design itself. Use them on as many surfaces as you would acrylics, remembering that they are thinner. Latex paints are particularly nice to use if you want to match the wall color of a room exactly, or want to ensure that the colors you are using will blend properly with it. Either use the paint as is, or tint with acrylics for perfect coordination.

*Spray paints* can be used as you would acrylics, except that you may want to use more than one light coat. The main thing to remember about using spray paints is that you must be sure to leave a large margin around the cut areas, so that colors go only where you want them. You will also have to weight the stencil down or tack it in place with rubber cement to keep paint from seeping under edges and mixing with other colors. A loosely attached stencil results in a messy, blurred outline that is extremely undesirable.

While we are on the subject of various kinds of paint, let's discuss a common problem: surfaces that no paint seems to cover. Sometimes this is due to the extreme porosity of the surface. Other causes, are stains that refuse to budge. Our local paint dealer introduced us to a product that truly ends this nightmare. It is called Flash Bond #400W White Primer and Sealer produced by X-I-M Productsline in Westlake, Ohio. We have yet to find a surface that doesn't respond to it. We highly recommend using it on any problem surface.

*Marking pens, colored pencils, and crayons* are good choices for working out a stencil design on plain paper before applying it to wood, cloth, or any other intended surface. You might find that a color combination that you thought would be harmonious is, in fact, most disagreeable. You can work out a new color scheme on paper without having stenciled a piece that you wouldn't be happy with.

While we are on this subject, we would like to say a little more about marking pens. A new side of stenciling is actually open due to some of the new, improved pens that are available. There are a large variety to choose from, the most readily available being Magic Markers, Flair pens, and Bic Bananas. We find that the most satisfying of any to use, however, are Design ® Markers by Eberhard Faber, Inc. The pens are available in three nib sizes: regular, pointed, and ultrafine. The regular nib is available in ninety-six colors, the others in forty-eight. They dry instantly and beautifully with a perfectly even finish regardless of the size of the space covered—a drawback with all other markers.

Some aspect of stenciling with a marker are identical to stenciling with paint. For instance, using a wide pen to go around the edges of a stencil may very well cause seepage. With the Design ® Marker you can go around an edge with a pointed nib and fill in with a regular pen in the same color. Blending is invisible and the results are beautiful. You will be able to use these markers on a variety of surfaces. In addition to most papers, they are excellent for clay flowerpots, stones and rocks, and paperweights.

## Brushes and Other Coloring Tools

*Stencil brushes* are blunt-ended brushes that come in a large variety of sizes and with a varying degree of stiffness of bristle. These brushes are inexpensive, comfortable to use, and cover quickly. The larger sizes, however, do not allow as much control over working as we would like. Stencil brushes are especially preferable for very large designs or designs of one-color as might be put on a floor. For such projects we recommend a No. 40 303 Delta.

*Artists' brushes* are also something you should have on hand to do the work that a stencil brush cannot. Brights are preferable, but flats are also good and will produce fine results. These brushes, like stencil brushes, are inexpensive.

It would be wise to have a basic assortment of

stencil and artists' brushes on hand for stenciling. We recommend the purchase of Grumbacher stencil brushes Nos. 00–3. You will find that No. 0 and No. 3 are the ones you will use the most. You should also have a No. 8 on hand for filling in larger areas once the edges have been taken care of with a smaller brush. In addition to these stencil brushes, round out your collection with a couple of brights, preferably Grumbacher 626B No. 10 and 4567B No. 10, and you should be ready to tackle almost any project you desire.

*Velour or flannel patches* wrapped tightly and neatly around the tip of your index finger and then dipped in paint, blotted, and dabbed on will produce great results. As unorthodox as it may sound, it is a sure way to develop lovely stencils with subtle shadings. We enjoy this method and use it often. It is, however, a bit messier than brushwork. If you want to be fastidious about it, you can cut a finger from a rubber glove and use it as a finger protector.

*Sponges* can be used to fill in stencils as well. Cut the sponge into small pieces, dab in the paint, and apply. In addition to coloring-in, the sponge will produce an interesting, mottled texture.

*Rollers* are often used for stenciling very large design areas. You might consider using them if you are doing a floor or a whole wall. Be sure to use very small amounts of paint and blot the roller on a piece of newspaper before applying paint to any surface to ensure that you won't be dripping paint and ruining your piece. It is easier to apply a second or even a third thin coat than it is to repair or redo a sloppy first coat.

## Miscellaneous Materials

In addition to the materials already mentioned, you will need a few other supplies for stencil work. These include tracing paper for sketching designs, masking tape for securing stencil material for cutting and painting, newspaper or paper toweling for blotting paints before applying, transparent tape for repairing stencils, a piece or pane of glass approximately 12-inches square for cutting out acetate stencils, and a ruler for measuring and marking out the placement of designs.

This takes care of materials. In the next chapter, we will discuss how to put all the items collected to their very best use.

# CHAPTER TWO

# Design Tips and Techniques

## Choosing Designs

WE ARE EXTREMELY proud of all of the designs that have been created especially for this book. You will be able to trace them easily and use them immediately as is, or you can enlarge or reduce them, or alter them in any other way necessary to suit your own needs.

You may, however, find that there is a design you particularly want to stencil that is unique to your own home or life-style. Perhaps you would like part of an upholstery design reflected on a wall or a wallpaper design carried over to curtains or throw pillows. Whatever the need or interest, it can most likely be adapted for stenciling. Let's take a look at design possibilities other than those contained in the Design Portfolio.

Animals, birds, and flowers are always favorite motifs among craftspeople regardless of their specialty, from needlepoint to woodworking, and, of course, to stenciling. All such "designs from nature," as well as leaves, trees, nuts, vegetables, and shells, are easily adaptable from pictures or from the real thing. More about how to adapt a stencil design from a picture later. To use actual flowers and leaves as stencil material, all you have to do is press them flat and dry them for a week to ten days and you should have a good, usable stencil. Seashells will often work, provided that they are fairly flat with an interesting outline.

In searching for design ideas, look for things that illustrate your personal interests. Perhaps you have a favorite workspace, retreat, or den where you retire to pursue special hobbies or organize collections. Why not personalize such an area with stencil designs that reflect your interest. Decorate walls, floors, curtains, desk, or chairs. Whether your interest is trains or teapots, you can display it in stencils along with your special collection. In our own homes, we have each stenciled our craft work areas with designs representing spools of thread, skeins of yarn, various needles and hooks, baskets and all the other paraphernalia of the crafts we enjoy.

Another popular theme for stenciling is to letter a message or saying on a plaque that is decorated with a few other fanciful designs. The possibilities here are vast. Consider a nameplate for the front door or a child's room. Or try a one-word message like "EAT" or "LOVE." You can also letter entire mottoes or proverbs. And don't forget items like mailboxes and welcome mats.

Perhaps a particular period of art or history attracts you, or your home is decorated in a definite period style. You can adapt all the styles to stenciling, including art deco, art nouveau, and op art. Paper doilies used as stencils will produce designs reminiscent of those wonderful, Victorian antimacassars. Tape down or use rubber cement to hold the doily in place, then spray-paint, and remove the doily when the surface you are stenciling is completely dry.

Various ethnic motifs are also excellent sources of stencil designs. Mexican, Latin American, and North American Indian weaving designs are beautiful as stencils, as are the peasant embroidery patterns of central Europe and Scandinavia. Far Eastern batiks and delicate Japanese designs are also marvelous. Primitive sculpture with its angular lines and ingenuous designs are wonderfully suitable for stencil. You can easily adapt an African mask or sculpted piece. Pennsylvania Dutch hex signs are also a popular design source.

Design possibilities, as you can already see, are unlimited. All that you need to keep in mind is that you will be breaking a design down to its simplest reproducible elements. Pieces of extreme complexity or intricacy become difficult, if not impossible, to reproduce exactly. Yet, you should be able to adapt and reproduce enough of any design to make pleasing and recognizable companion pieces to their original sources.

## Stencil Bridges

Let's say you have just found a picture of a bird that you want to stencil. You take a piece of tracing paper and trace it, and the result is a solid shape. In order to get more than this solid shape, you will have to alter the design and create details. Such details in stencils are known as bridges. As the name suggests, they are the areas of uncut stencil left between the cut-out design areas. In addition to helping to create detail and style, bridges are what hold a stencil together on one piece.

In order to create bridges in designs you choose, start by tracing the desired object. Next add a second line about 3/16 of an inch away from the first line and you will have broken the design down effectively. Once you get more proficient, you may decide that one area needs a wider or narrower bridge, or you may add bridges for extra detail that were not present in the original.

## Enlarging and Reducing Designs

Sometimes after choosing and bridging a design, you will find that it is either too large or too small for your purposes. Enlarging or reducing a design to your specifications is no problem. You can either take it to be photostatted or do it yourself using the square method.

A photostat is, of course, the simpler method. All you need to do is look in the classified pages of your phone book—usually under the heading of photocopying. Then take the design itself or a tracing of it to the company. Tell them how much bigger or smaller you want it and in a short while you will have a design scaled perfectly. The cost is usually small for this service.

The square method is free and you don't have to go any further than your own desk, but it can take a bit longer than having a stat house do it for you. If you've attended public school any time within the last forty years, you have probably learned it. *To enlarge*, take a design and trace it. Mark off the tracing every quarter to three-quarters of an inch (depending on the size of the design) along the length and width. Join the marks with lines and you should now have a design covered with squares or a grid. On a separate sheet of tracing paper mark off a similar set of squares. In this case, the number of squares will be the same, but their size will be larger. If you want your design twice the size of the original, double the size of the grid square, for three times the size, triple it, and so on. For other proportions, just figure out the mathematics and sketch the boxes accordingly. Once the second grid is drawn, transfer the original design to it by copying it box for box.

*Reducing a design* is accomplished by reversing the process. Instead of plotting larger squares on the second grid, draw a grid that is proportionally smaller than the one covering the original design. Then transfer the design, box for box.

## Kinds of Stencils

Once a design is selected and ready for transfer to stencil material, a decision must be made as to what kind of stencil you will want to use. There are three kinds of stencils that you can cut. Let's take them one at a time.

*One-piece stencils* are those with the entire design cut into one piece of stencil material. Such a stencil is most efficient for one-color designs. You can use more than one color with these stencils, but great care must be taken to prevent your brush from accidentally covering neighboring cut-outs in the stencil. To help prevent this, you can use a smaller brush for edges and a larger one to fill in.

*Register stencils* are used for designs that will have two or more colors. If you want a piece to be yellow, green, and red, you would then cut three stencils: one with the yellow areas cut out, one with only the green areas cut out, and the third with just the red design areas cut. Each stencil would then be marked with ink or notched on top, bottom, and sides (these marks or notches are called "registers") so that each stencil piece can be lined up perfectly with the others. Additionally, you have to mark the lines of each previous stencil, using a broken line to avoid mistaking

*Trace a design and draw a grid of equal size squares over it. (See A). To enlarge it, draw another grid with the same number of squares, but of a larger size. Copy the design lines box-for-box from the original (see B). To reduce the design in size, do the same thing, having the second grid consist of squares that are smaller than the original ones.*

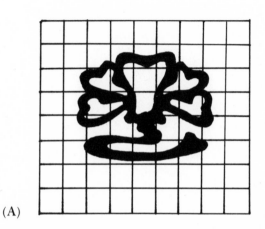

(A)

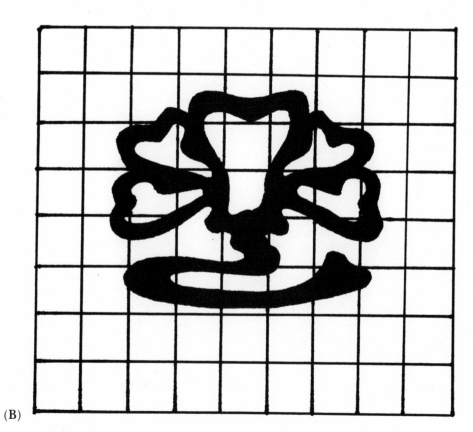

(B)

*If you plan to do a design all in one color, the simplest thing to do is to cut a one-piece stencil. Simply trace and cut it exactly as you see it printed.*

Often you will want to work a stencil in more than one color, or you will want to simplify it just to eliminate difficult cutting, or both. Here is the one-piece stencil from page 17 broken down for a register stencil. The first stencil (A) incorporates some of the petals and details with none close enough to each other to complicate painting or cutting. Note that the remaining parts of the design are marked with a dotted line so that the pieces of the stencil can be easily aligned. The second stencil (B) features the remaining design elements with the details of the first stencil in outline form.

A.

B.

*Beginning stencilers should advance their cutting techniques in stages. Novices should start with simple curves and straight lines as shown here. Remember that a simple design need not result in stencils that are any less lovely.*

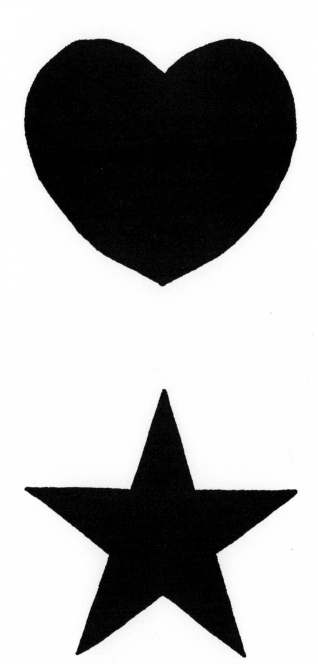

Intermediate stencilers can try more complicated designs with smooth circles and long curves as shown here.

Once you gain some experience with cutting, you will be ready for advanced work with designs as intricate as this one. The important thing to remember is not to try to do more than you're ready to. Practice will bring expertise.

them for cutting lines. All you need to do when painting is to match the registration marks.

A second use of register stencils is that designs can be broken down to such small components that bridges are actually eliminated. Some stencilers will use six, eight, or even a dozen or more stencils to create a design which when finished will look as if it has been painted by hand.

*Component stencils* are those whose various pieces are cut separately. If the design is a bowl of fruit, one stencil might be the bowl itself, another a banana and apple, yet another would be a bunch of grapes. Broken down in this manner, you can rearrange the pieces and change the whole design as often as you like. Another advantage of such stencils is that they are time-savers, particularly at cutting time. If you are cutting a stem with many leaves, or a flower with many petals, all you need to cut are a couple of leaves and petals. Then just reuse them along the stem or around the flower center. Component stencils are also practical for borders, repeat, or allover patterns, rather than cutting one large stencil.

## Preparing and Cutting Stencils

After determining the design and the kind of stencil you will use, the next step is to cut the stencil. You will need the traced design, stencil material, a cutting tool, and a piece of glass on which to cut.

Tape the tracing to a piece of glass that is large enough to cover it with a two- or three-inch margin all around. Use masking tape for this. Also tape the edges of the glass all around just to prevent any potential accidents due to splintery edges.

Next, cut the stencil material to size. Plan a two-inch margin all around. It will not only make for a stronger stencil, it will also help to keep things neater later, when it's time to paint. With a nice wide margin, you don't have to worry too much about paint sloshing over the sides and edges of the stencil and getting onto the surface of whatever you are stenciling. Now lay the stencil material over the glass and secure it with masking tape.

You are now ready to begin cutting. The traced stencil under the glass will serve as the key. Do not expect perfect results the first time, but be assured that after a few practice pieces you will have mastered stencil cutting. It is not difficult, but rather a matter of getting the feel of how it is done. When cutting remember these very important points:

* * Make sure that the blade on your cutting tool is sharp. Cut lines should be made in single, clean strokes. A dull blade will prevent you from making such strokes and produce ragged lines.
* * Hold the cutting tool as you would a pencil and keep it perpendicular to the stencil material.
* * Always be sure to cut toward yourself. Turn the stencil, not your arm and hand.
* * Cut with a steady pressure. You should be cutting easily through the stencil material and not rubbing the glass too hard.
* * Keep the cutting blade on the traced line in order to avoid distorting the design.
* * Take care not to cut beyond the end of a line.

These instructions were specifically geared toward using acetate or another clear plastic as a stencil material. There is really very little difference in procedure if you are using an opaque material. Instead of tracing a design and taping it to glass, you will need to transfer the tracing directly onto the stencil material. Do this with carbon paper, or use the old standby of going over all of the lines on the back of the tracing with a soft lead pencil. Then place the tracing right-side up on the stencil material. Go over all of the lines, applying pressure with a soft lead pencil. When you lift the tracing, you will find that the lines have transferred. Let the method you use be determined by the surface of the stencil material. If you transfer using the pencil method, you might want to go over the trace lines with ink to make them easier to see and cut. When cutting you will not need the glass. Simply secure the traced design to a piece of cardboard or other similar surface—ceiling tiles are good. Then cut out the design.

Once the design is cut from whatever stencil material you use, hold the stencil up to the light or

When cutting a stencil from acetate, first apply masking tape to the edges of the glass plate. Then trace the design and tape it right on to the glass.

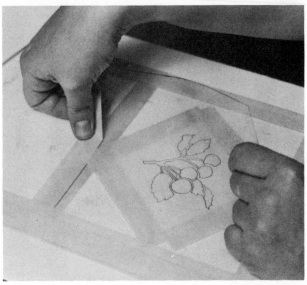

After the tracing is secured to the glass, tape down the acetate right on top of it, taking care to cut the acetate larger all around than the design you will be cutting.

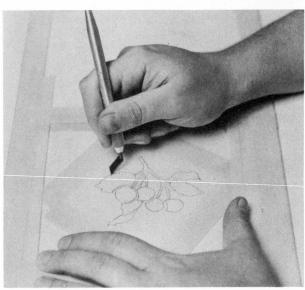

After tracing and acetate are firmly secured to the glass plate, you can begin cutting out the stencil. Here a Grifhold No. 113 is doing the work. Note that you always work toward yourself as shown. When necessary, turn the design, do not try to twist your arm or wrist.

against a window. Examine it carefully for ragged edges, broken or sliced-through bridges, and overcut lines. If you find that the stencil you have cut is too messy, try again. Many beginners are overcautious and apply too much pressure and cut too slowly, continually lifting the blade from the stencil to see what they've done. This results in a very tired arm and wrist and a poor stencil. Try to relax—use your arm naturally and smoothly and lift the blade as little as possible. Practice is the key word. You will simply have to "try and try again" until you feel that you are producing adequate stencils.

## Repairs

Even the most expert stencilers occasionally make mistakes and slice through a bridge or overcut a line. Or sometimes a rather delicate bridge will break after repeated use. This should not be regarded as a tragedy. If it occurs, just take small bits of tape—Scotch Magic tape doesn't become sticky or gluey after using—and apply the bits to both sides of the torn area. Use your cutting tool to remove excess tape.

If a piece breaks off completely from the rest of the stencil, it is still salvageable, but will require a little more work. Cut a replacement piece from additional stencil material. Tape it in place on the broken stencil, securing both top and bottom with tape. Cut away excess tape and the stencil should be as good as new.

## Care and Storage of Stencils

Stencils need only a minimum of care to remain in good working order. Clean them thoroughly after each use, checking to see if any repairs are required. If so, attend to them right away before storing.

When storing stencils, do not pile them on top of each other or stuff them into one big box or envelope. Rather, place each one in a separate envelope. A large letter file is an excellent container, making storage and separation easy.

You can mark each envelope with either a verbal description of the stencil—"cherries and leaves"—or stencil the design itself on the outside.

With this small amount of care, your stencils will last and serve you well. Your small investment of time will be well worth it.

## Color Tips

All color combinations from subtle to bold, from ingenuous to sophisticated can be worked into fine stencil designs. Many people find it difficult to choose colors. Here are some suggestions if you are stuck when making color choices.

One way to get an idea of whether or not the colors you have in mind work is to try the design on paper using crayons or marking pens. This way, you can try as many combinations as you like before going on to stenciling a finished piece.

If you find yourself at a loss for even choosing a group of colors to work with, turn to the color wheel. We offer one here in black and white. You can probably get one at your local paint store where they are offered as giveaways. We also have discovered that color wheels are featured in the large mail-order catalogs. We often refer to one in the interior decorating section of the J.C. Penney

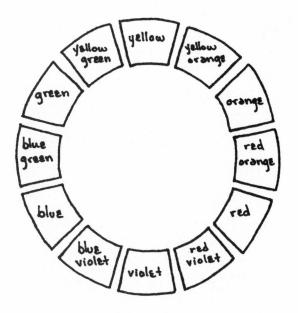

catalog. There are three basic color schemes: monochromatic, analagous, and complementary. Monochromatic means that you use just one color in various shades and tints. An analagous color scheme incorporates colors that fall next to each other on the wheel—red, red orange, and orange, for example. A complementary scheme uses colors that are opposite each other on the color wheel: blue violet and yellow orange are one example.

Monochromatic colors can be very subtle and rich-looking, while a complementary scheme can be sharply defined and contemporary.

Remember with stenciling that a background color must also be taken into consideration. Choose one that will provide enough contrast with all of the colors in the stencil design. Also, bear in mind that black and white as backgrounds can dramatize and highlight designs. Use darker colors with white and light ones with black backgrounds.

## Painting Tips and Techniques

When you are ready to apply a stencil design, there are a few things to remember about how to use the brush and apply color.

* * Dip just the tip of the brush into the paint.
* * Always use a fairly dry brush. Remove any excess color by blotting the brush on paper towels or newspaper. A drier brush will help to prevent paint from seeping under the stencil to areas where you don't want it.
* * Start painting on the margin of the stencil itself and proceed to the cut-out areas. This will help make a smooth transition and add to cleaner edges.
* * Do not use the kind of strokes for stenciling that you would for ordinary paintings. Fill in colors by holding the brush as perpendicular as possible and tapping it up and down, make good use of the brush's blunt edge.
* * Make sure that the stencil is well-anchored and hold it down with your

fingers around the areas you are coloring in. This extra holding helps prevent uneven edges and makes a nice clean outline. If you are stenciling around a very narrow bridge, use a toothpick or other small pointed tool to hold it down as you color.
* * Paint outer edges before filling in the center of the design.
* * If you are using register stencils, be sure to clean off the paint frequently to avoid obscuring register marks and design outlines.

As with any other area of stenciling, practice will quickly develop a beginner into an expert painter. Do not be faint-hearted. The very first piece we painted on was an absolute disaster. The design was to be a hearts and flowers peasant motif in red and blue, splashed all around the frame of a mirror which had been painted yellow. The first element to be stenciled was a large red heart in the center of the top side of the frame. When the stencil was removed, our hearts sank, along with the excitement at having discovered a new craft. The mirror was put aside and we began to work on pieces that we came to call sampler boards. We quickly regained our enthusiasm and stenciling has become an extremely rewarding pastime along with our other craft interests.

Remember with painting that a certain amount of naivete and imperfection are an inherent part of the beauty and appeal of stenciling. It is not an exact art, nor is it meant to be. If some small part of a design is not perfect, don't worry—the overall effect of a finished piece will be beautiful.

## Sampler Boards

One of the best ways we have found to work out designs and color schemes is with sampler boards. To make one, get a plain unfinished piece of scrap wood. two feet by three feet is a good size. Paint background colors in various shapes. Then try out designs, color schemes, antiquing toners. You can get a good idea of how something will look before you put it on a piece.

In addition to providing an excellent place to practice, these boards can become attractive decorative pieces in their own right. And they will serve as an invaluable "reference library."

## Repeat Patterns, Allover Patterns, and Border Designs

Various projects that you design for stenciling will have repeat patterns, allover patterns, or border designs. They are all easily handled with just a few guidelines.

Basically you can treat repeat and allover patterns in a like manner. Since you will be using the same design again and again, it is a good idea to cut several stencils of it. This way you can apply paint to four or five elements at a time. By the time you are ready for the next one, the first stencil should be dry and you can remove it and begin again. Also, be sure to clean stencils between each application. If you don't, you are just asking for trouble. A small amount of paint that may have seeped under the stencil and caused no damage on the first application can smear and ruin a design if the stencil is reused.

Border designs can be handled like repeat patterns until it comes time to turn a corner. To do this, you will need to match the edges of the two design pieces. First, lay down a strip of masking tape at a forty-five-degree angle to the border design. Make sure to use a piece long enough to intersect the border design itself. Color in the stencil as usual and continue right onto the tape when you reach it. After the paint dries, pick up

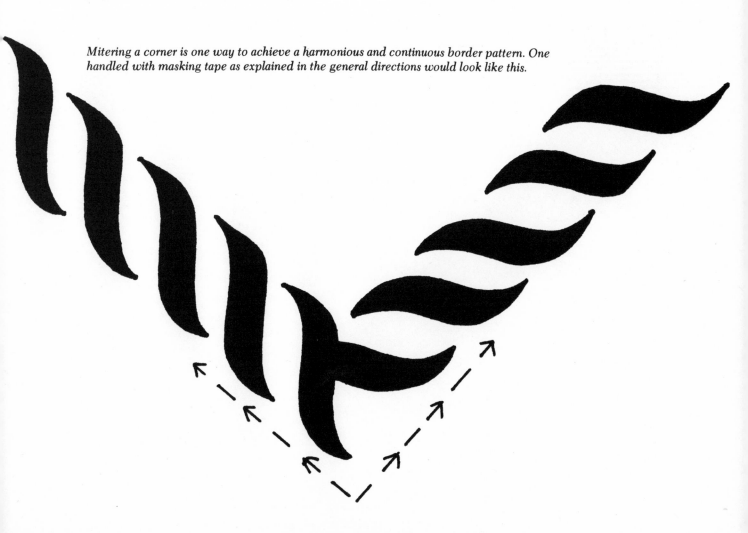

*Mitering a corner is one way to achieve a harmonious and continuous border pattern. One handled with masking tape as explained in the general directions would look like this.*

*Another way to treat corners when working a border is to change the stencil direction at an obvious focal point of the design as shown here.*

*If you are a little more adventurous, you might try inventing a corner treatment that fits in with the natural flow of the design as we did here.*

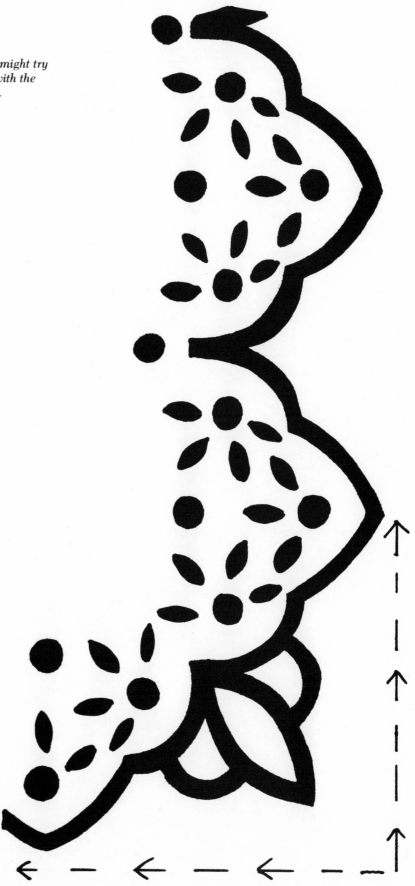

*Yet another way of dealing with corners is to use an element of the design at an angle at the point at which you wish to turn.*

the tape and lay it down again, this time so that its edge fits exactly into the edge of the design that is already stenciled. Now stencil the next part of the border, again coloring right on the tape at the point of intersection. After it dries and the tape is removed, you should have a perfect corner.

## Correcting Painting Errors

Smudges and other small mistakes can be covered up after the rest of the stenciling is completed. Simply dip a fine-tipped artist's brush into the background color and touch up around the edges as needed. For this very reason, it is always a good idea to keep a small amount of background color in reserve. Also remember that with such minor mistakes, a blade, a kneaded eraser, even a bit of tissue wrapped tightly around your finger can often remove unwanted bits of paint that have not had the chance to dry.

Seepage and the misplacement of stencil designs are two other common problems that stencilers encounter. They are actually handled in the same way as the smaller errors. If you catch the mistake while the paint is still wet, try removing the paint immediately with tissue, blade, or kneaded eraser. If the paint has already dried and the seepage or misplacement is not too awful, try repositioning the stencil so that its new edge is just enough removed from the existing one to be repainted and correct the error.

If seepage or misplacement is so severe that no amount of touching up or fiddling will help, your only choice is to wipe off what you have done and start again. Check to see what solvent is necessary for the paint you've been using, remove the unsatisfactory area, and repaint the stencil.

With the material in this and the previous chapter, you are now well-equipped to begin stenciling. The chapters that follow will cover particular information for stenciling on various surfaces from wood, to brick, to food and fabric.

Your stencil craft adventures can now begin in earnest.

# CHAPTER THREE

# Stenciling on Wood

STENCILING ON WOOD is probably one of the most popular forms of the craft. And for good reasons: wooden articles are readily available, painted wood surfaces can accommodate some of the most beautiful and interesting designs. Stenciling can transform a tacky old table or a worn-out desk into the star attraction of a room. It is a wonderful way to give new life to a moribund article of furniture that would otherwise be destined for the attic or the dump.

Almost all of the articles that we stenciled for this book are examples of such restorations. The children's table and chair belonged to us when we were children; we salvaged it out of our mother's attic. Other pieces, such as the sewing cabinet, were "inherited" from family or friends. The lovely desk was left behind in an apartment that friends of ours moved into. We saw its potential, removed the old, dark mahogany finish, and created a delicate and beautiful piece.

Start keeping an eye out for likely stencil candidates. Check thrift shops, yard sales, and even the town dump. You'll be amazed at how many things you'll be able to acquire and redo with little or no out-of-pocket expense.

## Preparing Wood for Stenciling

If the piece you are planning to stencil is old and battered, or is coated with thirteen plies of paint, you will want to begin by getting down to the original wood or finish. Get as close to it as your own energy and the quality of the piece of furniture to be stenciled merits.

If the surface is fairly smooth and not heavily painted, you can begin by washing the whole piece down with a mild cleaner such as Glass Plus by Texize. It will remove a wealth of sins, without harming the wood. Follow this rubdown with a light sanding and use a tack cloth on all of the ouside surfaces. Test for bleeding (see page 44) and you are ready to apply the base coat.

Some people prefer an absolutely smooth, bare wood from which to start. With an old, scratched, nicked, and dented piece, this will mean stripping it completely to remove all layers of paint and/or wood finish, and then sanding until nothing but the smooth, wood grain remains. Basically, you have two options: having the stripping done for you by a professional or doing it yourself. Obviously, the first saves time and energy and eliminates the chance for making mistakes, but it will cost you. The second option is easier on the pocketbook, but tough on one's often little-used arm muscles and can take anywhere from hours to days depending on the size of the piece and the amount of stripping that is required. Commercial stripping preparations come with instructions and there are many excellent books available on the subject.

One of the things to note regarding stripping and sanding is that a base paint plus stencil designs will often hide the most serious flaws that an old piece of furniture might have. On the other hand, some of the nicks and scratches acquired through age and use can lend a certain charm to the finished stenciled piece. This is, of course, a matter of personal taste and judgment. Our own preference is to maintain the "lived-in" look on the pieces we work on.

The important thing is to have a fairly smooth, oil- and dust-free surface on which to work. Once you have it, the next step is to apply a base coat of paint for the stencil design. We have used quick-drying latex paints with various finishes (satin, low-luster, flat—but never high-gloss) exclusively for this. You can use oilbased paints as well, but we find the end result no more gratifying, and with the longer drying time required for oilbased paints, not to mention a much more difficult clean-up, they just do not seem to be worth the effort.

In applying the base coat of paint, there are two things to keep in mind. If the piece you are painting requires more than one coat of paint, make sure that the first one dries thoroughly, then sand it lightly and use a tack cloth before applying the next coat. Secondly, if the piece has a veneer, finish, or wood stain, test a small area with the base paint first to see if it "bleeds through." If it does bleed, it may take three or more coats of paint before you'll be able to get a good cover. In this case, sealing the piece with shellac before applying a base coat is preferable. The same holds true for old wood or new wood that might be very porous and therefore drink up the base coat as you apply it.

Many people like to use the commercially available antiquing kits that come with a base paint and a toner that provides that antiqued look. These are perfectly fine for stenciling, too. Just remember that you should not apply the toner immediately after the base coat dries as you would if you were simply antiquing the piece. Instead, apply the base coat, let it dry, then apply the stencil design and let it dry. Finally, apply the toner over both stencil and base coat.

## Applying the Stencil

When stenciling on wood, you may use the stencil material of your choice for cutting the design. Secure the cut-out stencil to the piece you are working on and you are ready to color it in. Follow the guidelines in Chapter Two to apply the color.

## Color

Choosing a harmonious blend of colors is another area of personal taste and judgment. We have already discussed the basics of color blending and color schemes in Chapter Two. Here we will make recommendations as to what kind of paint you should use to color in your design.

Our top choice for coloring-in wood stencils is acrylic paint. It is easy to use, can be thinned if necessary, and it is easily removed if some disastrous error is made. They are also very fast drying. We cannot recommend them highly enough.

You can also use japan paint or enamel paint. There will be nothing wrong with the results, but the application is harder—they are sloppy to work with. It is also more difficult to clean up and to repair mistakes without having to begin all over again. In addition, both are considerably more expensive than acrylics.

If you are particularly concerned with matching colors to a room or its wallpaper or upholstery, you can prepare your stencil colors by tinting the latex base coat with acrylic paint. This ensures a perfect blend every time. It is, in fact, exactly what we did to get the color blend on the desk. The colonial blue of the base coat was tinted with blue and yellow to get the green, while reds and purples were used for the rest.

If you have decided to paint a floor and stencil it, a good choice of paint is patio or deck enamel. It is a paint designed for heavy wear. It really doesn't need any further protection on the surface. Remember that these paints are slow-drying—you must allow forty-eight hours drying time. This means that you will want to avoid overlapping stencils unless you are prepared to wait the necessary amount of time between colors. Use either a random design, or one very large simple pattern that contains a few repeated motifs. We would like to add that although no further protection is required with this paint, we have found that a coat or two of polyurethane will add to the life of a stenciled floor.

## Final Touches

Once the stencil is applied and dried, it is time to apply antiquing stain or toner, if you are planning to do so.

One or more coats of polyurethane or varathane should nicely protect and preserve your work. You can buy either with a gloss or a matte finish depending on the particular look that you want.

You can also use shellac with equally good

After you decide how much toner you want to remain, make sure to wipe it evenly off of the entire area. By working on the sampler board as we have here, it is easy to see the difference in the finished effect of using toner or simply stenciling the design and then coating with polyurethane or other protective coating. When you approach the actual piece of furniture, it will be with a sure knowledge of how it will look when finished.

After a design is applied and has dried thoroughly, apply the antiquing toner thickly, using either cheesecloth or paper toweling as an applicator.

Here, a bit of a pattern has been applied to a board and is about to be antiqued. It is a good idea to work out such test pieces before moving directly to the furniture itself. This design was actually the beginning of the antique sewing cabinet featured both in this chapter and in the color section.

After applying the toner, begin to rub it off, again using cheesecloth or paper toweling. Rub away a small amount at a time, until you achieve the desired degree of shading.

results. White shellac will produce a transparent, shiny finish. Orange shellac is also transparent, but will add an old-fashioned air that is often interesting. This is in fact the substance used to give decoupaged articles that antique look. Before going ahead with orange shellac, test it over the base coat on a scrap of wood or on some unobtrusive spot on the piece. You want to make sure that you'll like the effect it produces. It would be a shame to have come this far and end up with a piece you didn't love.

Whether you use polyurethane, varathane, or shellac, determine the number of coats you will give the finished piece by the kind of wear you expect it to endure and survive. For example, you may want to give a well-traveled floor or something to be used by children as many as three coats. A picture frame would not need more than one coat.

Now that the piece is painted, stenciled, and preserved, the only thing left for you to do is to select a place of honor for it in whatever room it is expected to enhance. Then go off in search of a piece for your next project.

## HOW-TO
# Wood

Following are step-by-step directions for a number of wood items. They are representative of the various methods used and the different problems you might encounter from antiquing to handling a real problem piece to working on oddly-shaped surfaces such as window moldings. We realize that it is unlikely that you own the exact same pieces of furniture that we do, but chances are that you might own something similar or that you will someday come across a slant-top desk or round table in which case our designs and methods will be of great help to you. In any case, most of the designs are easily adapted to any piece of furniture. Of course we've only suggested a few uses of stenciling on wood here. Your own imagination will supply many other projects—like stairs, radiator covers—almost anything that's made out of wood.

*A front view of the antique sewing cabinet.*

*Top of antique sewing cabinet.*

# SEWING CABINET

## Materials:

screwdriver

Benjamin Moore's Benwood Heritage One-Day Antiquing Latex Base Coat in Teal #234-31, or color of your choice

acetate

Grifhold No. 113 knife

glass

masking tape

tracing paper

Grumbacher acrylic paints in red (cherries), thalo green (leaves), raw sienna and burnt sienna (stem)

small stencil brushes (Nos. 0 and 1)

Carver Tripp's Antiquing Toner, color No. 1602 Dark

Flecto Varathane Liquid Plastic Clear Satin No. 91

cheesecloth or paper toweling for applying toner

brushes for applying base coat and varathane

1. Remove all hardware from furniture with screwdriver.
2. Prepare wood surface according to instructions in this chapter, or have the piece stripped professionally.
3. Apply the teal base coat and allow to dry thoroughly, applying a second coat at that time if necessary.
4. Trace a stencil design from the Design Portfolio and cut a stencil from acetate following the instructions given in Chapter Two. Since this is an allover pattern, you will want to cut several (about four or six) in order to make the painting go faster.
5. Apply stencils in a pattern that is pleasing to you. We followed the contours of the cabinet (see illustrations) but a completely random placement would also work nicely. When applying stencils, mix the two siennas in equal amounts for the stems. Be sure to clean stencils between applications.
6. Cut out a border stencil from the Design Portfolio. Apply the accent stencil to the cabinet's legs using red acrylic paint (see illustration).
7. When stencils have dried, apply the toner in a fairly heavy coat and rub away with cheesecloth or paper toweling until the desired effect is achieved (see photographs for a step-by-step description of this process).
8. When the toner has dried, apply two coats of varathane, making sure that the first coat dries thoroughly before you apply the second one.
9. Replace hardware and drawers.

Because this particular type of sewing cabinet is commonly found in homes, grandmothers' attics, yard sales and antique stores, we are showing how to place the design in some detail because we are certain that many people will want to duplicate it. This page (top) sketches the cabinet top. Print double cherries one inch from the edge midway at front and back. This page (bottom diagrams the large drawer. Center double cherries midway between the holes for the drawer knobs.)

back

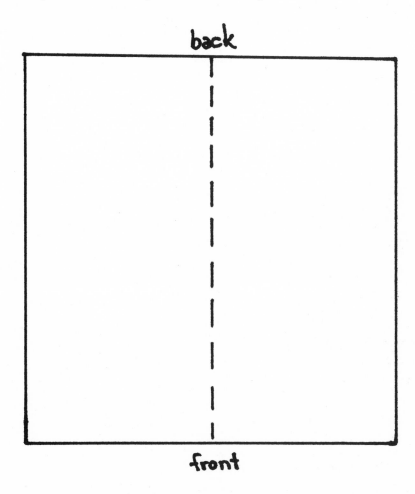

front

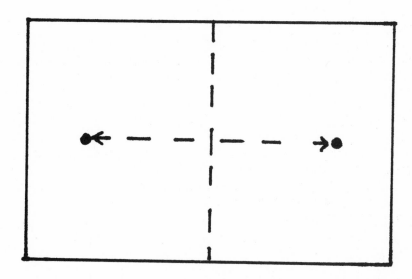

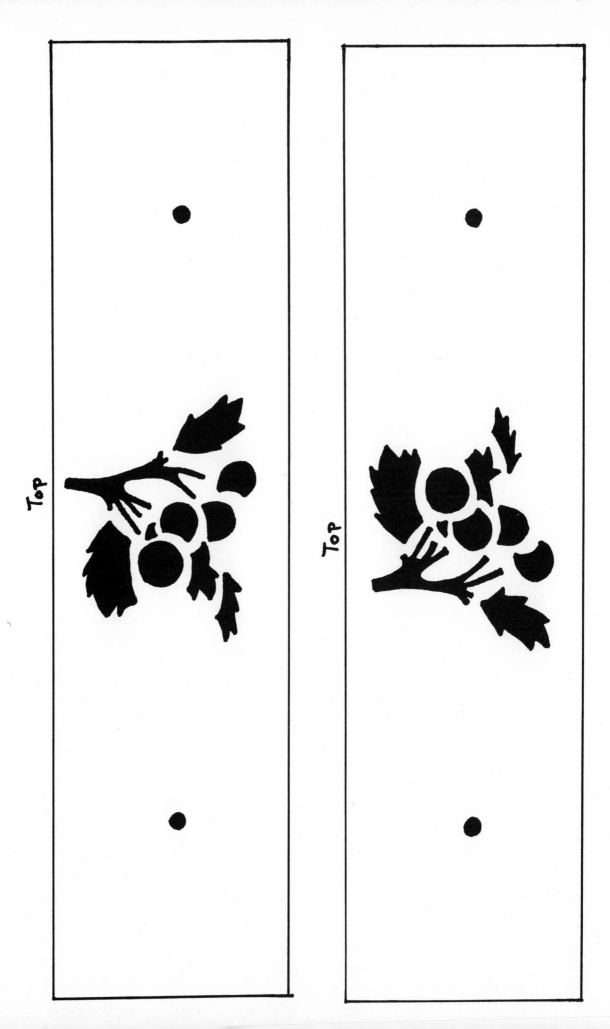

*Stencil the small drawers as shown, placing the cherries midway between the knobs and pointing in opposite directions from each other.*

TOP

TOP

On the front of the sewing cabinet, the accent stencil design continues up to the top and all around the bottom, following the direction of the arrows.

*Stencil the upper sides (hinged) as shown here.*

*This child's table is a charming piece in the tot's bedroom or play area.*

*Simple decorative accents were used to decorate the chair that accompanies the child's table.*

# CHILD'S TABLE AND CHAIR

<u>Materials:</u>

Carver-Tripp Latex color Low Luster Enamel 8004—Carriage Red
acetate
tracing paper
glass
masking tape
Grifhold No. 113 knife
chalk
Grumbacher acrylic paints in yellow, green, gray, white, orange, pink
small stencil brushes (Nos. 00–1)
Flecto Varatane Liquid Plastic Clean Satin No. 91
brushes for applying varathane and base coat.

1. Prepare wood surface according to instructions in this chapter, or have the piece stripped professionally.
2. Apply the carriage red base coat and allow to dry thoroughly, applying a second coat at that time if necessary.
3. Trace the designs of your choosing from the Design Portfolio. Cut acetate stencils according to the directions given in Chapter Two, making separate stencils for each of the motifs.
4. Find the center of the table by drawing horizontal and vertical chalk lines connecting the center points of each side. Draw a ten-inch circle in chalk for placement of the elephants. Mark positions of the remaining figures, each about one and a half inches from the edges of the table and evenly spaced along the edge—for our table they were three and a half inches apart.
5. Secure the stencils with masking tape and color them in, apply the central motif first, then the borders. Color in stencil on chair (see illustration).
6. When the stencils are completely dry, apply two coats of varathane, making certain that one coat is completely dry before applying the second.

Make one stencil seven inches long with a tulip at each end. Mark a dotted line in between connecting them and mark the midpoint as well. These lines will serve as a base line for the other motifs along the border and also pinpoint their position.

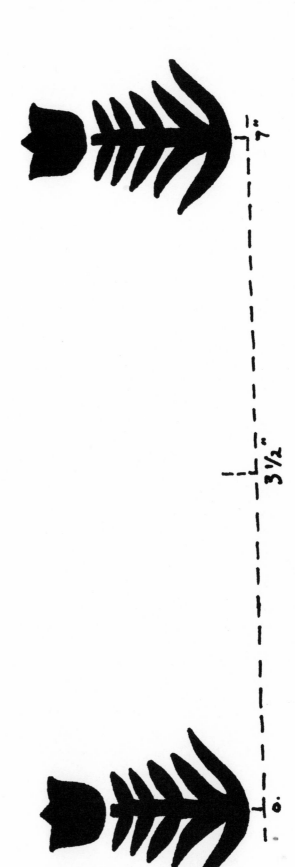

*Left:*
*Decorate the spindle with various sized hearts. The center heart is blue, the top and bottom hearts are bright green and the remaining two are bright yellow.*

*Right:*
*Mark the center of the top back part of the chair with a dotted chalk line. Reverse the direction of the motif on either side of the dotted line. The colors of the motif reflect the colors on the spindle with the central motif of each side painted bright blue, the outer ones bright green and the inner ones bright yellow.*

*This graceful-looking desk was once a rather dull and heavy old mahogany piece. The pigeon-hole interior is lined with hand-marbleized paper in delicate and complementing colors.*

# SLANT-TOP DESK

## Materials:

screwdriver
Benjamin Moore's Latex Paint in Wedgewood Gray
chalk
stencil paper
tracing paper
X-acto knife
cardboard
masking tape
Grumbacher acrylic paints in alizarin crimson, hansa yellow, and white
small (Nos. 00-1) and medium (Nos. 2-4) stencil brushes
polyurethane
brushes for applying polyurethane and base coat.

1. Remove drawer knobs and drawers. With a screwdriver, unfasten hinges holding the slant-top in place and remove slant-top.
2. Prepare the wood surface according to the instructions in this chapter, or have the piece stripped professionally.
3. Apply Wedgewood gray base coat and let dry thoroughly, applying a second coat at that time if necessary.
4. Mark the center of the slant-top with chalk for placement of the central design. Mark a point with chalk three inches in diagonally from each corner. These marks are for lining up the corners of the design.
5. Trace designs of your choosing from the Design Portfolio and transfer to stencil paper as described in Chapter Two. Then cut out the stencils also following the instructions in Chapter Two.
6. Mix acrylics with the base coat as follows to produce blended shades of pink and green: add small amounts of alizarin crimson and white to the Wedgewood gray to produce several shades of rose and pink; use hansa yellow and white and the base coat to produce several greens. Paint stencils starting with the central motif, then do the borders (see illustration), and finally apply the feathery design to the drawers (see illustration) and to the top of the desk (see illustration).
7. When the stencils have dried, apply two coats of polyurethane, making certain that the first coat is completely dry before applying the second.
8. Replace hinges, slant-top, and drawer knobs. Put drawers back in place.

When applying the feather motif to the top of the desk, mark the exact center of the top with a dotted chalk line. Have half of the motifs going in one direction, then clean the stencil and position it so that the motifs on the other side will point in the opposite direction.

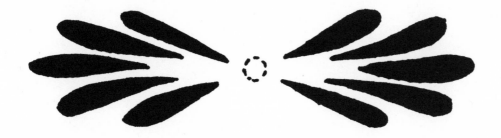

When applying the design motif around the drawer knobs (dotted circle) use it first in one direction, clean it thoroughly and then apply it facing the other way.

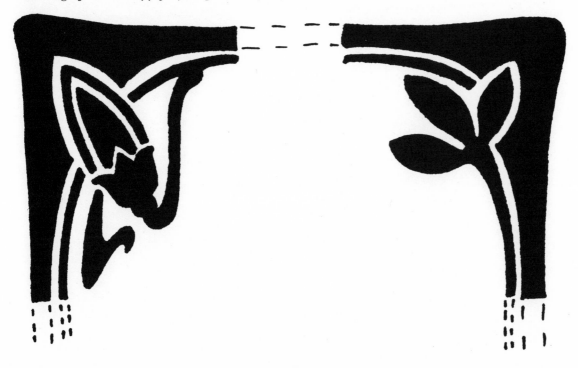

In applying the borders it will be necessary to extend the connecting lines of color from corner to corner. Draw dotted chalk or pencil lines to use as a guide and then paint them in.

The central motif.

*This wooden window frame was enlivened by the addition of a stenciled border. Note how the pattern is worked out from the bottom center.*

# WINDOW MOLDING

## Materials:

Benjamin Moore's Regal Aquaglow in Colony Yellow

acetate

Grifhold No. 113 knife

glass

masking tape

tracing paper

Grumbacher acrylic paints in red and green

medium stencil brushes (Nos. 2–4)

brush for applying base coat

1. Prepare wood surface according to instructions given in this chapter.
2. Apply colony yellow base coat and allow to dry thoroughly, applying a second coat at that time if necessary.
3. Trace stencil design from the Design Portfolio and cut an acetate stencil according to the instructions in Chapter Two. Make a strip of at least eight motifs in order to expedite painting.
4. Paint in stencils, alternating red and green. Follow illustration for bottom center. Due to the curved construction of the molding, you will have to hold and guide the stencil with your free hand to prevent seepage and maintain clean, sharp edges.
5. Allow the stencils to dry thoroughly. There is no real need to further protect the surface due to the very limited use and handling it receives.

*Mark the exact center of the bottom part of the window molding with chalk lines. Work the design up to it facing in one direction, work away from it with the design facing the opposite way. At the very center create an 8-petaled flower by repeating the middle of the design facing up and down on the dotted line as shown.*

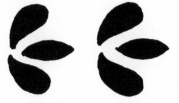

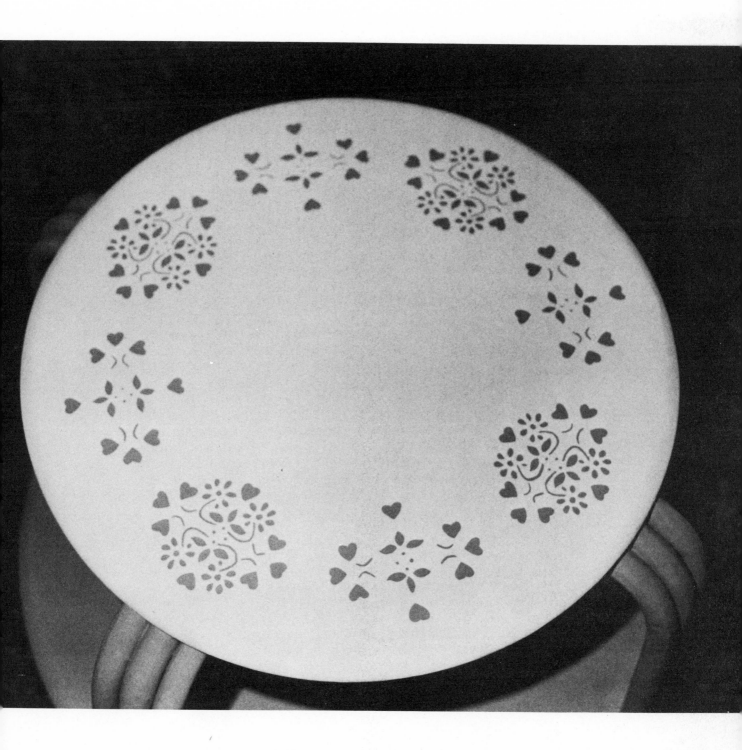

This table was one of the biggest problems we have ever dealt with. After removing several layers of paint and finishes, we discovered wood so badly stained, that no paint covered the imperfections. It was Flash Bond that remedied the situation and enabled us to finish the piece.

# ROUND COFFEE TABLE

## Materials:

sandpaper

Flash Bond #400W white Primer and Sealer

flat white latex paint

Sapolin Latex Flat Paint 5/M/114 (or similar Celery Green)

stencil paper

tracing paper

cardboard

masking tape

X-acto knife

small stencil brushes (Nos. 00–1)

polyurethane

brushes for applying primer and sealer, base coat, and polyurethane

*Note:* This particular table was inherited from a friend who was about to throw it away. He had inherited it himself when his parents were throwing it away some years before. After removing several coats of paint, we discovered a surface with several stains that nothing seemed to cover. Our directions are therefore written in terms of a piece with a problem finish. If your round piece has no special flaws, simply prepare the surface according to the general instructions given early in this chapter and continue from Step 3.

1. Sand surface until smooth.

2. Apply two coats of Flash Bond primer and sealer, making sure that the first coat has dried thoroughly before applying the second.

3. Apply white base coat and let dry thoroughly, applying a second coat at that time if necessary.

4. Trace a design from the Design Portfolio and transfer to stencil paper according to the instructions given in Chapter Two. Cut stencil using the X-acto knife, also following instructions in Chapter Two.

5. Secure stencil with masking tape one and a half inches from the outer edge. Paint in the design with green paint. When dry, remove and clean the stencil thoroughly. Lay the stencil down to the right of the completed design and repeat. Continue around the table until the border is completed. Make sure that the designs are evenly spaced around the table's circumference, this will depend on the size of the table you are working on.

6. When stencils are dry, apply two coats of polyurethane making sure that the first coat has dried before applying the second.

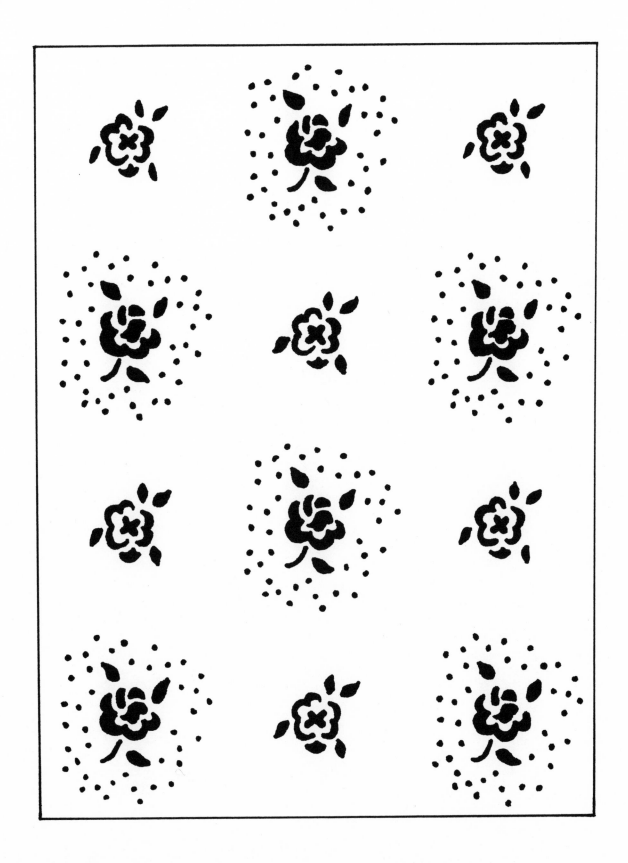

# CHAPTER FOUR

# Stenciling on Fabric

STENCILING IS ONE way to personalize your wardrobe. Items of clothing can be monogrammed, trimmed with a decorative design, or even stenciled with an allover pattern.

Of course, fabric stenciling is by no means limited to your wardrobe. A particularly lovely thing to do is to stencil curtains or drapes with a design picked up from the wallpaper or upholstery in a room. You can also turn plain white sheets and pillowcases into designer originals with the addition of a stencil pattern. The possibilities are almost endless. Generally, if you can think of it, and it's made of cloth, you can stencil it. You can stencil handbags, hats, window shades, pillows, lampshades, placemats, napkins, tablecloths, dish towels, scarves, men's ties, blouses, skirts, lingerie, sneakers, wall hangings, luggage, umbrellas, curtains, potholders, even tennis racquet covers!

## Choosing and Preparing Fabric

Practically any fabric is suitable for stenciling. You can do it on all of the natural fiber materials such as denim, cotton, silk, wool, chiffon, canvas, hopsacking, cotton suede, sailcloth, taffeta, burlap, felt, kettle cloth, monk's cloth, and flannel. Most of today's flat knit fabrics are also perfectly fine for stenciling, as are most of the synthetics, including dacron, polyester, acetate, tricot, antron, quiana, and ultrasuede.

Fabric color and texture do not present any great problems either. Light and dark colors can be stenciled with almost equal ease, as can either thick or thin fabrics. Textures will often add dimension and interest to a design. Printed fabrics, especially in plaids and checks, can often form a basis for an interesting stencil design as well.

The only caution we advise is that you avoid using any fuzzy mohair-like fabrics or anything with a deep pile. Also steer clear of bulkily or loosely woven fabrics. The stencil if it takes at all over such fabric will not be as beautiful as it would on something more tightly woven.

There is actually very little to do as far as preparing fabric for stenciling. Although it does not have to be new, the fabric should be clean, dry, and completely free of wrinkles. If ironing at home does not remove the wrinkles, then have a dry cleaner do it for you.

## Applying the Stencil

When stenciling, the fabric should be held as taut as possible. You might want to pin it down to a board or place it on a canvas stretcher or in an embroidery hoop before beginning if you think you won't be able to manage it using just your hands. We've also secured fabric successfully with masking tape. First, cover your work surface with paper toweling, then tape the fabric right onto the surface.

If the fabric item you are stenciling has more than one layer, as a T-shirt, place several thicknesses of paper toweling, newspaper, or a piece of cardboard between the layers to prevent the colors from soaking through.

If you need to mark special guidelines for the placement of the design, mark them with tailor's chalk which can be easily brushed or rinsed away when the stenciling is completed.

We recommend using acetate stencils for working on fabric. You won't have to worry about paint ever soaking through the stencil material and the transparent acetate is a real asset. Anchor the cut stencil in place with scotch or masking tape and you are ready to begin coloring in the design.

## Coloring

You have a choice of coloring materials when stenciling on fabric. You may use acrylics (our favorite), high-gloss enamels and oil paints in combination, textile paints, or cold water dyes.

Acrylics are fine for all washable fabrics. You can use regular artists' acrylics right out of the tube. Some companies also produce special fabric acrylics. We like them best because we find them to be the easiest to apply. They also can be thinned easily with water in order to adapt to the fabric being stenciled. A rule of thumb to follow is that the heavier or thicker the fabric, the more you can, or should, thin the paint. It's much better to apply two or even three thin coats than to have one thick layer of paint. The latter will just look thick and sloppy, while several thin layers will result in an even, attractive design. One note on the use of acrylics: avoid using them on any fabrics that say "dry clean only." They're just not able to withstand dry cleaning without breaking down or cracking.

High-gloss enamels and artists' oils can be used on any fabric. There are no restrictions as far as the cleaning of the stenciled piece. Once dry it may be either dry cleaned or machine washed. You must remember, however, that these paints are meant to be used in combination only. The enamels are used in primary colors (red, blue, and yellow) and the oils are added to the enamels to create a spectrum of colors.

Using these paints is a lot trickier than using acrylics, but once you get the hang of them, the end results can be quite stunning. If you do plan to try using them, you will also need a jar of mineral spirits to thin them. Remember when using the oils from the tubes that you should use only a small amount at a time. One-half to three-quarters of an inch is more than enough. They will stay usable out of the tube for quite some time. To create the various colors, just use the tube paint added to the enamel. In working on dark-colored fabrics (discussed more later in this chapter), you may need a white base coat on which to build. Test a small piece of the fabric to see if the color is covering. If not, mix white enamel and white oil paint in equal amounts and use it as a base. Stencil in the desired colors when the base coat is dried.

Textile paints are perfect for fabrics that require dry cleaning, but they can also be used on washable fabrics. As a general rule, they should never be thinned unless you are stenciling on a highly absorbent fabric like terry cloth. The use and preparation of fabric paints vary greatly from manufacturer to manufacturer, so you will have to take careful note of the specific instructions accompanying any brand that you might purchase. We've found that if you follow the manufacturer's directions without trying to take shortcuts or assuming that what goes for one brand also goes for another, you should not experience any great problems. We also would like to recommend an excellent beginner's kit of a six-jar assortment of paints from "Skylight Studio."

Cold water dyes are suitable for washable fabrics only. To stencil with them, you will also need to purchase dye thickeners which are used to make the ordinarily watery dyes thick enough to paint with. As with the other coloring agents, dyes can produce beautiful results, but they are tricky to work with. For one thing, they cannot be used on dark-colored fabrics. Dyes are in fact transparent, so you will lose them on any but white or light-colored surfaces. You must also bear in mind that the background color of the piece you are stenciling will blend with the dye color and give you a new color (except, of course, with a white background). For example, yellow on blue will produce green, on a red background it will turn orange. Red on blue will produce purple. Of course, the shades you get will vary depending on the shade of the background fabric and the color dye you use. The color blending aside, you will also have to be concerned with setting the dye and removing the thickeners once the piece is completed. Here as with the textile paints, procedures vary from manufacturer to manufacturer and you will have to follow the specific directions that come with the brand you purchase.

Regardless of the coloring agent you ultimately choose, there are a couple of things to remember when stenciling fabric. One is to test the color on a scrap of fabric so that you can get a feel for the proper working consistency of the color. In fabric stenciling, you don't want merely to coat the surface, but you will need to force the paint down into the weave of the fabric. With a little practice you will find the right consistency. Basically you do not want to apply too thick a coat of color. Heavy paint build-up is ugly and can also affect the permanence of the stencil design.

Use thin coats. If you don't cover the first time, apply a second thin coat. Tap your brush up and down and use a circular motion and additional pressure if necessary, to force the paint down into the weave of the fabric.

Another thing to bear in mind is the procedure for working on dark-colored fabrics. Since colors may not show up as vividly as you might like them to in just one or even two coats of color on a dark background, it is a good idea to start a design on dark fabrics with a single layer of white. Let the white dry and then build the stencil design on it.

## Final Touches

Once a fabric piece has been stenciled, there is not a great deal to do. If it is an item that can expect to see some heavy wear such as seat covers, sheets, or cushions, you might want to spray the finished piece with Scotch-gard to help protect against dirt and stains.

Also, because the finished pieces can be washable and/or dry cleanable, this does not mean that they should be treated as indifferently as an old pair of blue jeans. Stenciled fabric pieces should receive the same careful attention as any other piece of treasured handwork.

To give a washable piece its longest life, do not

*Attention needleworkers: You can use stencils for embroidery, crewel work, and needlepoint. Simply transfer the design to cloth or canvas and color in with needle and thread.*

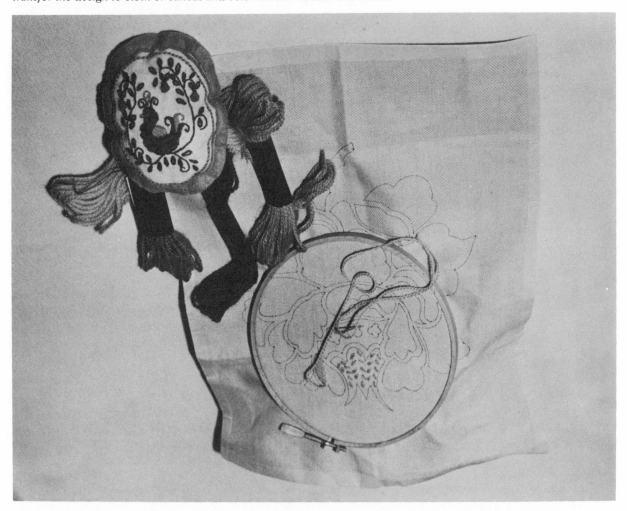

subject it to the wear and tear of a washing machine and drier. Rather, handwash it with whatever soap is suitable for the fabric. Then, let the piece drip-dry or let it dry flat without wringing out. Wringing can be too punishing and it can definitely shorten the life of the piece. If the article needs pressing after it dries, iron the painted areas on the back only and be sure to use a press cloth.

As for dry cleaning, any competent dry cleaner should be able to do a good and thorough job on stenciled fabric.

### A Word to Embroiderers and Needlepointers

Most stencil designs are suitable for regular or crewel embroidery and to needlepoint. All you need to do is transfer the stencil to cloth or canvas and then fill in with stitchery instead of paint. It's a lovely way to accent existing designs or stencils.

A friend of ours has stenciled the moldings in her living room with a design picked up from her wallpaper and upholstery. Then she stenciled the same design on some cotton and stitched up some throw pillows in crewel. The results are fantastic with so many different textures and substances coordinated by a single design.

### HOW-TO

# Fabric

The following are projects suitable for work on cloth. You can use them exactly as we direct, or use the idea and substitute a design of your own choosing. Also remember that although we give directions for baby T's the same rules would apply for children's and adult T's as well. Tablecloths and napkins are always welcome gifts, and something like the Victorian pillow takes on an heirloom quality. Stenciling on cloth is sure to be one of your most rewarding stencil experiments.

This director's chair cover is patterned after Guatemalan folk weaving designs. The bird also appears on the sweatshirt featured in this chapter. Note how a different use of coloring can create quite a different-looking creature.

# DIRECTOR'S CHAIR COVER

## Materials:

acetate

tracing paper

Grifhold No. 113 knife

glass

newspaper

masking tape

new or freshly laundered back piece for director's chair

tailor's chalk

Grumbacher acrylic paints in titanium white, yellow ochre light, red oxide, and
cadmium orange (these last two mixed in equal parts)

small stencil brushes (Nos. 00–1)

1. Trace designs from the Design Portfolio. Cut acrylic stencils according to the instructions given in Chapter Two.
2. Cover your work surface with several thicknesses of newspaper. Lay the cover—which should be wrinkle-free—flat on the newspaper with inside surface facing up. Secure with tape or pins.
3. Using tailor's chalk, mark off lines to follow for borders and for the placement of the central motif.
4. Paint in the stencils. Paint the central motif first, then the border, taking care not to apply the paint too thickly. Be sure to clean the stencils between applications. When dry, apply additional paint to cover if necessary.

*Mark the diagonal center of one edge of the napkin with tailor's chalk. Place the stencil on that center line about 1 inch up from the corner. See Gold Harvest Napkins illustration (page 85) for more detail.*

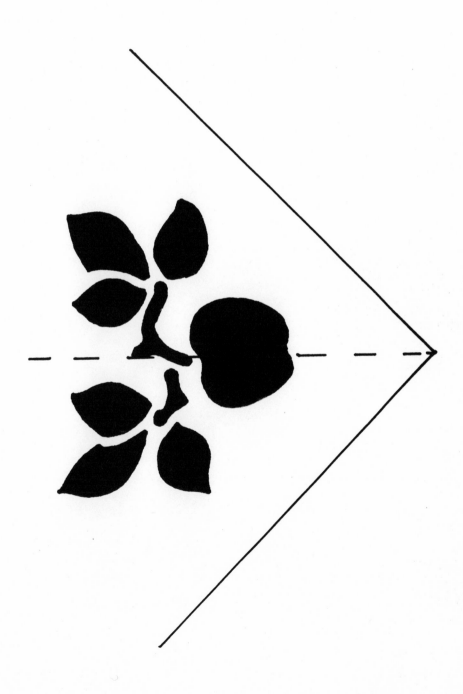

# OVAL TABLECLOTH AND NAPKINS

## Materials:

acetate

tracing paper

glass

newspaper

masking tape

Grifhold No. 113 knife

one fringed white oval tablecloth and matching napkins, either new or freshly laundered

Grumbacher acrylic paints in bright red and bright green

small stencil brushes (Nos. 00–1)

1. Trace a design from the Design Portfolio. Cut six to eight acetate stencils following the instructions given in Chapter Two. (*Note:* You can do this project with just one or two stencils, but the job will go much faster the more stencils you have.)
2. Press cloth and napkins so that they are completely wrinkle-free.
3. Cover work surface with newspaper. Lay a napkin flat and secure with tape or pins. Using the illustration as a guide for placement, secure the stencil in one corner of the napkin and paint in the design. Repeat with the remaining napkins, taking care to clean the stencil thoroughly between applications.
4. Lay the tablecloth flat—the larger your work surface, the faster this will go. Tape all stencils down at once and secure with masking tape. Place each one and a half inches up from the fringe and space them evenly apart as you work around (this dimension will depend on the exact size of the cloth you are decorating). Paint in stencils. When they are dry, clean and retape them. Proceed around the cloth in this manner until the border is completed.

*Stencil a matched set of tablecloth and napkins for a truly lovely gift to yourself or even to someone else!*

# BABY T'S

## Materials:

acetate

tracing paper

glass

newspaper

masking tape

Grifhold No. 113 knife

3 infant's (0–3 months) T-shirts, one yellow, one aqua, one light green

acrylic paints in soft colors

small stencil brushes (Nos. 00–1)

artist's brush No. 000 (for yellow T)

1. Trace designs from the Design Portfolio.
2. Cut acetate stencils following instructions given in Chapter Two.
3. Spread newspaper over the work surface. Lay down one T-shirt front side up and slip newspaper between the two layers of the shirt.
4. Tape stencil in place on the center front of the shirt.
5. Paint in stencil taking care not to coat the shirt too heavily. If necessary, apply a second light coat to cover. For the yellow T-shirt, paint in the polka dots on the mouse's dress with the artist's brush after the rest of the design has dried.

*These infant's shirts make wonderful gifts. Notice that we have used these designs elsewhere with very different effects.*

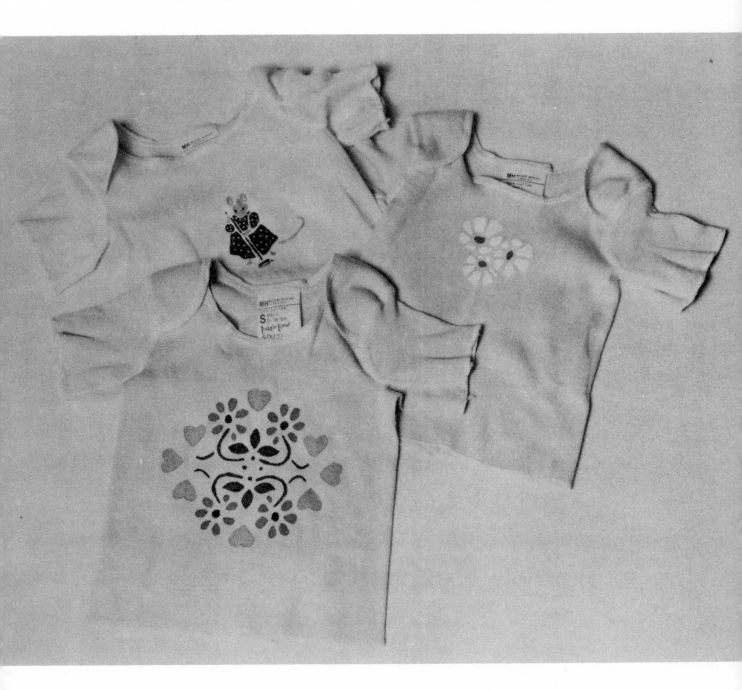

# VICTORIAN PILLOW

## Materials:

2 pieces of brushed cotton denim, in a neutral shade (we used a mushroom beige), each 15-inches square

stencil paper

newspaper

cardboard

X-acto knife

tracing paper

acrylic paints in soft, dusty colors

small (Nos. 00–1), medium (Nos. 2–4) and large (Nos. 5–6 or larger) stencil brushes

thread to match fabric

¾ yard heavy cotton lace edging, 2½ inches wide, in an off-white

polyester or dacron pillow stuffing

1. Make sure that the fabric is wrinkle-free, pressing carefully if necessary.
2. Trace a design from the Design Portfolio and transfer to stencil paper following the instructions given in Chapter Two. Cut the stencil also following the instructions in Chapter Two.
3. Spread work area with newspaper. Lay one fabric square down right side up, and secure with masking tape.
4. Center the stencil on the fabric and secure with masking tape. Color in, taking care not to coat too thickly. Apply a second thin coat to cover if necessary. (*Note:* We used a combination of dusty roses and greens.)
5. When the design is dry, finish the pillow as follows. Pin the fabric pieces together with the lace edging in-between. Make sure that you have the fabric squares with right sides together and that the fabric and lace edges are all flush with each other. Machine-stitch all around, making a half-inch seam and leaving about four inches open along one side for stuffing.
6. Turn pillow right side out. Push out corners with the point of a pair of scissors.
7. Stuff pillow. Hand-sew opening closed. Hand-sew lace edges together.

*This stenciled pillow has a Victorian look to it. Different trim and a boldly-painted design would result in a very contemporary-looking one.*

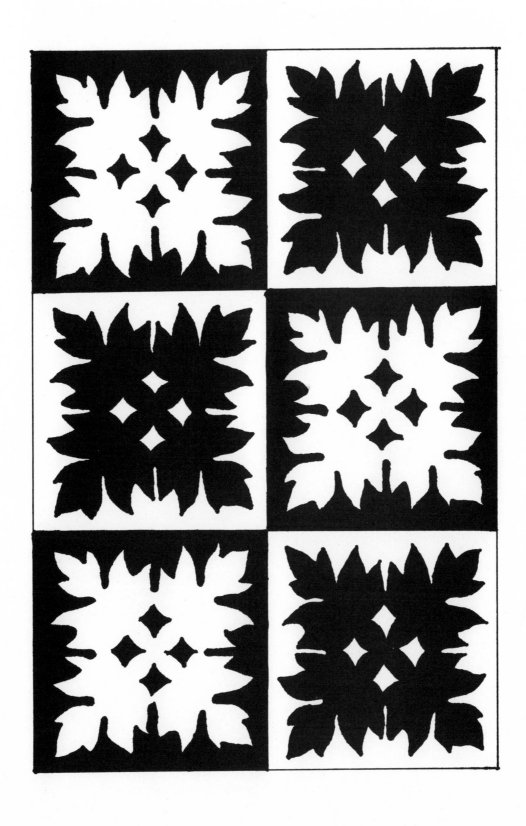

# CHAPTER FIVE

# Stenciling on Food

THERE IS NO greater way to impress guests than by serving them dishes of great beauty. Most hostesses rely on colorful garnishes—ornately arranged sprigs of parsley, lemon wedges, bits of tomato or pimiento, radish roses—or on handsome serving platters. Others will go to great lengths creating veritable sculptures of confections atop desserts and cakes. There is no question that unique decoration and presentation can turn even the plainest dish into a feast for both eye and palate.

Few people, however, are aware of the glorious things that can be done using stencils on food.

## Food-on-Food

This type of stenciling is great fun and something that even children can easily produce. You should start with a base of about a twelve-inch square fruit and nut loaf. Spread the top with an even layer of cream cheese. Lay the desired stencil on top and fill in the cut-out areas with bits of finely chopped food—nuts or raisins. Or you could begin with a plain chocolate or white cake, topped with a smooth layer of frosting. Stencil a great big flower and fill in with coconut flakes, cherries, bits of chocolate, or chopped up lemon bits. A nice touch for a children's party is a clown stencil decorated with fruits, chocolate chips, nuts, jelly beans, or cinnamon hearts.

For a grand addition to a buffet table remove the crusts from ordinary white, rye, and pumpernickel breads. Spread each slice with a spreading cheese—use several different kinds—or herb butter. Plan small stencil motifs and fill in with olives, pimientos, capers, nuts and seeds, chopped celery, carrots or hardcooked eggs, anchovies, caviar. The possibilities are endless and the results are always gorgeous.

The only guideline you need keep in mind is that frostings, butters, and cheese spreads should be smoothed off carefully—use the side of a knife or a spatula, skimming the top slowly and easily as you work your way across. Also let the spread surface set a bit before stenciling. You might even refrigerate for a half-hour or so before stenciling. When it is set, press the foodstuffs lightly into the surface. After you remove the stencil, let set again before serving.

Another nice hors d'oeuvre or buffet table treat doesn't even involve spreading anything. Just get an eight-ounce brick of cream cheese or any other soft cheese of a similar consistency, place your stencil design and sprinkle with fresh ground pepper, paprika, or finely chopped parsley.

## Sugar Stencils

Yearly bake sales don't have to result in cakes covered over with dense, sweet icing. Give others a special treatment: place a doily on the top of a cake and sprinkle confectioners sugar ever-so-carefully over it. When the doily is removed, a most elegant cake will be revealed.

We remembered that old process when it came time to put this book together and we can vouch for the fact that it works just as well as ever. Not being limited to doilies or confectioners sugar, you can turn out much more elegant and sophisticated-looking treats. Create any kind of stencil you choose, many from the Design Portfolio would be perfect—and don't forget that you can letter a message as well. In addition to the old standby confectioners sugar, you can fill in with colored sugar sparkles or candy confetti. One particularly sophisticated cake started as a plain angel food cake from a mix. We blended Dutch cocoa with confectioners sugar and sifted it on top—gorgeous.

The only special equipment you need for these

kinds of sugar stencils is a fine sifter. If you don't have a sifter, a fine-mesh strainer will do. Guidelines are simple: the stencil you use should be at least one inch bigger all around than the top of the cake. This allows for easy removal after sifting. Do the stenciling while the cake is still warm; it helps everything to stick a little better. If you must, turn the cake upside down in order to work on the smoothest surface possible. If you are decorating something like brownies or a spice cake that you will want to serve in squares, cut the cake up first and then stencil the individual serving pieces.

When stenciling with sugar, use very small amounts at a time. Sprinkle slowly and keep the sifter in motion using circular movements all around the cake to make sure that you are coating the surface evenly. If you hold the sifter about one and a half inches above the cake surface, you should be all right. Keep sifting until the entire surface is covered lightly and evenly. You will not be doing yourself or your guests a favor by trying to be generous with the sugar. The result will be a big mess without clear design edges. After you have sifted, comes the delicate job of removing the stencil. This must be done with special care to avoid ruining the design. The trick is to lift it straight up. Use two hands or even two people to pick it straight up off the cake. If you remove it at any kind of an angle you will smear the design. Just be very careful and you can be assured of beautiful results.

## Food Painting

To actually apply color to foods is clearly trickier than the two kinds of food stenciling we have already described. You can create some extraordinary-looking dishes, however, and will earn master points both as artist and chef.

There are two kinds of stenciling that can be used on baked foods. Either you can paint a design on rolled-out, unbaked dough or you can stencil a color design after baking.

In general, anything that you roll out gets stenciled before baking. This includes pie and strudel crusts, cookies and anything *en croute*

such as Beef Wellington. Things that bake and rise substantially and change shape are stenciled after baking. This includes most breads, cakes, and muffins.

As with all other stenciling, you will want to work on the smoothest surface possible. Always be sure to choose the smoother side of the rolled-out dough to color. Turn finished cakes upside-down if necessary. If you are baking your own bread, place the smooth side up in the pan to bake.

Something to note about bread for stenciling is that you do not have to be a baker to enjoy stenciling the product. You can purchase a freshly baked uncut loaf at a bakery and bring it home to stencil. There are also a number of commercial baking companies—Pepperidge Farm, for one—that offer uncut loaves which can be stenciled quite nicely.

In choosing a cookie recipe, use one that is fairly dense and that won't spread out a great deal in baking. Shortbreads are a good choice. As a rule of thumb, remember that recipes for cookies that are to be rolled out and cut with cookie cutters are usually formulated not to spread out while baking so as to maintain the cut-out shape.

There are two ways to handle coloring in food stenciling. You can use regular commercial food coloring diluted with water to the colors of your choice. These are excellent for most pie and cookie doughs. Apply the coloring with a fine tipped brush or a small piece of sponge.

Food coloring alone may not work on some doughs and cake surfaces. This is one reason to experiment with the dough you plan to use. If food coloring doesn't work, a special food "paint" will. To make food paint, use one teaspoon of water to one egg yolk and then add food coloring a drop at a time until you reach the desired color. Note that you don't get the range of color with food paint that you do with just food colors. The yellow of the egg yolk is the controlling factor. You won't be able to get a true red or blue. You can get various shades of orange, green, brown, and yellow—many of them quite beautiful. Apply food paint in the same manner as food coloring using a fine brush. An added bonus of using food paint is that the egg yolk creates a bright, shining glaze that makes the finished product look even more tempting.

Some other guidelines for working with food paint include the following:

* * When working with rolled-out dough for pies or cookies, press stencils slightly into the pastry.
* * Also on rolled-out dough, work sparingly with the coloring. Too much can cause unwanted seepage. It is better to build up a color. But also remember that too many layers of color can also mar a design.
* * If rolled-out dough starts getting soft while you are stenciling on it, put it in the refrigerator for ten or fifteen minutes before continuing.
* * When you have completed stenciling a piece of rolled-out dough, refrigerate it at once for about fifteen minutes or until it is firm. Then bake as usual.
* * Be careful not to pull or stretch stenciled unbaked dough too much, as when you are transferring a top crust from pastry board to pie plate. It can distort the design.
* * Should any part of the stencil design crack during the baking process, you can repair it easily with a bit more food paint applied to the problem area.
* * For baked breads and cakes, let them cool completely before doing any stenciling.

### Other Food Stencil Ideas

There are a host of things you can do with food coloring or food paint and stencils. We'll give you some ideas for inspiration and you're sure to come up with many more of your own.

You can make special occasion cakes by stenciling a message and/or a design on a large piece of cookie dough that can be placed right in the center of an iced and decorated sheet or layer cake.

Try serving up a stew on a brisk autumn day and top it with gaily-stenciled biscuits.

A decorative idea for luncheon sandwiches is to stencil the top half of the sandwich. Cut slices of bread in half either lengthwise or diagonally, and set aside. Toast and then spread an equal number of slices with cheese, tuna salad, or luncheon meats. Paint stencil designs on the cut pieces and toast very lightly. Place on top of the spread bases and serve. A variation for bridge parties is to quarter the slices and decorate with hearts, diamonds, spades, and clubs.

One final and delightful idea that is especially nice for children and the holidays is one that is fully edible. Make a batch of your favorite cookie dough. Take pieces and roll between your hands to create long ropes or snakes about a quarter- to half-inch around. Now fashion these ropes into various shapes—bells, snowmen, angels, candles. These shapes will be your stencils. Lay them on a well-greased cookie sheet. To color in, smash up colored hard candies, like charms or lifesavers, and sprinkle them into the open spaces. Bake at 350 degrees for about seven to ten minutes, or until the candies melt. When cool, lift off the baking sheets. These make lovely tree ornaments if you can refrain from eating them long enough to hang them.

## HOW-TO

# Food

A few ways to brighten up a table at an everyday meal or enhance a party buffet follow. Since most of this chapter has consisted of inspirational material, you can move on as your heart and appetite lead you.

# PARTY BISCUITS

<u>Materials:</u>

acetate

tracing paper

glass

Grifhold No. 113 knife

3 egg yolks

food coloring in red, yellow, and blue

fine-pointed artist's brush

12 pre-baked biscuits each about 1½ inches in diameter

1. Trace the designs of your choice, making sure that they are small enough to fit the biscuit.

2. Cut acetate stencils following the instructions given in Chapter Two.

3. Place each egg yolk in a separate dish. Add a teaspoon of water to each and mix up with a fork. Add ten drops of food coloring to each yolk and mix again. You should now have a vivid orange, a nice bright green, and a sunny yellow. Now mix a small amount of green and orange in another dish to make some brown.

4. Working on the smoothest surface of the biscuit, hold a stencil and begin to color in with the artist's brush. Apply several light coats if necessary, but avoid trying to do one thick coat. If the colors are not showing up enough after one or two light coats, add a few more drops of food coloring to the "paint."

5. Let the biscuits dry thoroughly and serve. The egg will provide a nice glossy finish that makes the biscuits even more appealing. Heating them in the oven wouldn't hurt, but don't actually bake them any further.

*Muffins stenciled with food paint are a delightful accent to a party table—or use them to dress up a humdrum meatloaf night.*

## PAPRIKA CHEESE

Materials:

one 8-ounce brick of cream cheese

waxed paper

sharp scissors

paprika

1.  Refrigerate cheese until quite hard.
2.  Trace a design from the Design Portfolio directly on to the waxed paper.
3.  Use a small, sharp pair of scissors to cut out the design, making sure to leave a border one and a half inches larger than the cheese all around.
4.  Lay stencil on cheese and press gently to make it stick.
5.  Sprinkle lightly with paprika and continue dusting lightly and evenly around the design until it is completely filled in.
6.  Carefully lift off the waxed paper, making sure to pull it up all at once, as described for sugar stenciling earlier in this chapter.
7.  Place stenciled cheese on an attractive dish and serve. Note that you can keep this cheese as long as you would an undecorated one, provided that it is covered and refrigerated.

*When stenciling foods such as these cheeses, extreme care must be taken when removing the stencil, otherwise the job is as easy as pie. That's paprika cheese on the left with pepper cheese on the right.*

# PEPPER CHEESE

Materials:

one 8-ounce brick of cream cheese

waxed paper

scissors

freshly ground black pepper

1. Follow Steps 1 through 4 as given for *Paprika Cheese* (preceding).
2. Sprinkle the freshly ground black pepper lightly and evenly over the stencil until the cut-out area is filled.
3. Cover the cut-out part of the stencil over with another piece of waxed paper and press gently with the palm of your hand to make the bits of pepper stick to the cheese.
4. Carefully remove the waxed paper covering, and then the stencil, making sure to pull it up all at once, as described for sugar stenciling earlier in this chapter.
5. Place on an attractive serving dish. As with the paprika cheese, this pepper cheese can be kept for as long as you would keep undecorated cream cheese. When refrigerating, make sure that the cheese is well-covered.

# CHAPTER SIX

# Stenciling on Paper

EVERYONE WHO HAS ever attended school in this country has no doubt stenciled on paper at one time or another. School science projects, posters advertising dances, picnics, and rummage sales, and bulletin board displays always seemed to require a trip to the local stationer to purchase several sets of stencil alphabets that came complete with numbers and punctuation marks, even some stars and moons if you were lucky or spent an extra few cents. And all in upper and lower case from a half to three inches high.

The art of stenciling on paper has not changed since our schooldays, but there is a lot more than lettering a sign for a local tag sale that you can do.

Personal and business stationery can be made to suit your personality and life-style. You will find that people are as excited by the design of your personal notes as they are over the news you have to share. Business stationery can be bold and aggressive or as witty or as straightforward as you desire. The important thing is that it will surely be eye-catching and that is a big plus in business— what catches the eye usually stays in the mind. If large designs or bold patterns do not appeal to you, remember that you can always create an attractive monogram for that simple, but elegant look.

Stenciling is also ideally suited to all kinds of cards. Honor Valentine's Day, Mother's Day, Father's Day, Christmas, Chanukah, Thanksgiving, Halloween, and St. Patrick's Day. And don't forget all of the other occasions when cards are appropriate—birthdays, anniversaries, weddings, graduations, engagements, thank-you notes, birth announcements, invitations.

Stenciling on paper also includes the whole realm of labels and special cards. Create lovely personalized labels for all of the jams, jellies, and other foods you enjoy preparing and storing or giving away. We use them on ours and in addition we stencil labels for the herbs and spices that we dry and keep and various liqueurs that we make. You might even consider stenciling a batch of cookies and wrapping and presenting them with a stenciled card. You can also personalize recipe cards, calling cards, place cards, book plates, and any other cards or labels that are prominently displayed or used as references or identifiers. We have also stenciled labels for ourselves and other craftspeople who use them as tags on the pieces they offer for sale. These handmade tags add an extra exclusive touch to the handfashioned items.

Gift wrap paper is another natural for stenciling, as well as a way of making a special gift even more special. You can decorate it with special occasion or seasonal motifs, or even create a wrap that is a distinctly personal message to the receiver. If you carefully cover just the top of the gift box, the paper will remain intact once the package is opened and the creative packaging becomes a gift in itself. And don't forget that you can forego using wrapping paper altogether and just stencil directly on to the surface of the box and lid.

For hard-to-wrap items, stencil a brown or white paper shopping bag, seal the top with decorative tape or ribbon and you've created a lovely package. Stenciling on newsprint is another way of creating an interesting gift wrap. You can make some pretty, unusual ones by using foreign-language papers—particularly Chinese, Arabic, Russian, or Hebrew, if they are available. The interesting characters of their respective alphabets form a wonderful background for inspired designs. Bear in mind that with all gift wrap projects, you can reproduce the wrap design or one of its elements on a card. The matching pieces will lend further distinction.

For a special party, it is great fun to stencil a paper cloth and plain white paper plates and cups. They can all bear a motif of the occasion being celebrated or reflect a specific party theme.

These have been just some of the many things that can be done with stencils on paper. Soon any blank paper will look bare and you will want to be stenciling everything from memo pads to grocery lists. Don't forget that you can also create great shelving paper and drawer liners, too.

*Shown here are two place cards for elegant entertaining, just one of the many kinds of cards that you can stencil.*

### Choosing Paper

The paper you use for any stencil project should be somewhat absorbent, though certainly not of the consistency of paper toweling. Most paper tablets, construction paper, cardboard, bond, parchment, watercolor paper, brown wrapping paper, and newsprint are all suitable. In general, you should avoid any paper that has a glossy surface or a metallic finish. If you have any doubts about the paper you wish to use, test a small piece with whatever you have chosen for coloring. You may have to change the coloring agent from marking pens to colored pencils, or you may even find that the paper is simply unsuitable for stenciling. In any case, a quick test will provide the answer.

### Coloring-in

There is a large variety of coloring materials that can be used successfully to stencil on paper: colored pencils, marking pens, watercolors, pastels, traditional school paint (also called tempera and poster paint), and, of course, the ubiquitous acrylics. It is a good idea to test the color on the paper you will be using. Apply inks, watercolors, and school paint with a watercolor brush or a small piece of sponge. Whichever you use, make sure not to have too much on the brush.

You will probably find that it is a good idea to apply a spray fixative to any of your stenciled paper pieces. It protects the design and gives the

paper a bit more body.

Sometimes after stenciling on paper, particularly if you have used watercolors or school paints, you will find that the edges of the paper tend to curl up. All you have to do to correct this curling is to press the piece right-side down on the ironing board with a dry iron.

So much for paper stenciling. We guarantee that if you get hooked on any part of this papercraft, you'll never look at another piece of paper in the same way again. And you will become your stationer's most favored customer.

**HOW-TO**

# Paper

Stenciling on paper is something most of us learned before we were even able to add or subtract. The projects here are fun to do and we are sure that you will think up many others of your own. And speaking of those early stenciling days, we have discovered that cutting out a few stencils and handing them over to youngsters with a box of crayons is an excellent rainy day project, as well as a way to keep them occupied almost any other time. The whole family can enjoy making cards and gift wrap and celebrating various holidays with stencil pictures.

*Here are three designs that are perfect for decorative labels. You can trace them directly from this page for use as stencils.*

Labels

Stationery can be personalized to reflect your mood and life-style. And even a dull letter will look interesting. We've worked up an art nouveau design (left) and a contemporary motif that is actually based on Guatemalan weaving.

## ART NOUVEAU STATIONERY

<u>Materials:</u>

acetate

tracing paper

glass

masking tape

Grifhold No. 113 knife

8½″ x 11″ white paper with good opacity

No. 10 (business size) envelopes

Eberhard Faber fine point marking pens in light and dark green

1. Trace a corner design from the Design Portfolio for the stationery and another design for the envelope.
2. Cut the stencils from acetate following the instructions given in Chapter Two.
3. Mark a point with a pencil one half-inch in diagonally from each corner of the paper. These will serve as guidelines for the placement of the corners of the design.
4. Starting in the upper left corner, match the corner of the design with the pencil mark and fill in with light green. You will have to hold the stencil in place with your free hand as tape might tear the paper. Repeat in the remaining corners, turning the stencil as necessary to fit in the corners.
5. We filled in our *fleur-de-lys* motifs with light green, placing them in the center of each edge and lining them up evenly with the corners.
6. We then placed the deco flower stencil on the extreme left of the front of the envelope and filled in with dark green.

# CONTEMPORARY STATIONERY

## Materials:

acetate

tracing paper

glass

masking tape

Grifhold No. 113 knife

8½" x 11" white paper with good opacity

No. 10 (business size) envelopes

Eberhard Faber fine point marking pens in magenta and turquoise

1. Trace design from the Design Portfolio.
2. Cut acetate stencil following the instructions given in Chapter Two.
3. Mark a dotted line in pencil a half-inch in from the left edge of the paper and from top to bottom.
4. Place stencil along this line and fill in alternating magenta with turquoise. Do not use tape to secure the stencil as it may tear the paper. Erase any pencil marks that show.
5. Mark a dotted line a half-inch up from the bottom edge of the envelope and use it as a base line for the stencil. Fill in as on the stationery. Be sure to erase any pencil marks that show.

*The stenciled gift wrap pictured was colored with acrylic paint. Velvet ribbons accenting the colors used add a special touch.*

## GIFT WRAP

<u>Materials:</u>

acetate

tracing paper

Grifhold No. 113 knife

glass

masking tape

plain white wrapping paper in whatever size is necessary for the package you plan to wrap (*Note:* You can also buy and stencil an entire roll of gift wrap paper and keep it to use on several packages.)

Grumbacher acrylic paints in cadmium orange and burnt sienna

small stencil brushes (Nos. 00–1)

¼-inch wide velvet ribbon in orange and brown to match paint colors.

1. Trace a design from the Design Portfolio and cut an acetate stencil following the instructions given in Chapter Two.
2. Lay the wrapping paper flat, weighing it down at the corners if necessary.
3. Follow illustration for placement of the allover design and color in the stencils, making sure to clean thoroughly between applications. You will have to hold the stencil in place with your free hand, as tape might either tear the gift wrap or mar its finish.
4. Wrap the package and tie with the orange and brown velvet ribbons used together as one.

*Place the design on even rows moving down and across. When you reach the edge of the paper, fill in as much of the design as will fit.*

*A gaily-stenciled gift box becomes a present in itself in addition to holding one.*

## GIFT BOX

<u>Materials:</u>

oak tag

tracing paper

X-acto knife

cardboard

masking tape

blue and white striped gift box with lid (We chose one with a mattress ticking pattern.)

Eberhard Faber fine point marking pens in red and green

1. Trace a design from the Design Portfolio and transfer to the oak tag following instructions given in Chapter Two.
2. Cut out the stencil with an X-acto knife, following the instructions given in Chapter Two.
3. Place the stencil at random around the box and fill in the design with the red and green pens. You will have to hold the stencil carefully with your free hand as tape might pull up the paper that covers the box.
4. Place a gift in the box. (We actually used ours for the oval tablecloth and napkins and gave it to someone dear to us.) Tie with ribbon. No further wrapping is necessary. The box will actually become a second gift as the person who receives it can use it as a decorative storage container.

# CHAPTER SEVEN

# Stenciling on Other Surfaces

Wood, paper, and cloth are probably the most commonly stenciled surfaces. The reasons are simple. We are used to seeing them stenciled and the surfaces are easily accessible to everyone. Every home has walls, floors, and old furniture that could use the cosmetic improvement of a stencil treatment. Everyone has a T-shirt or blouse that could be embellished. Everyplace we look there is paper to be had. We wrote about food stenciling in a separate chapter because of its interesting and unique nature. It is fun to do and just different enough to merit special treatment.

These four surfaces, however, are by no means the only ones suitable for stencil work. Practically any smooth surface can be stenciled provided that you use the appropriate materials. In this chapter, we will discuss many of the other stenciling possibilities.

## Stenciling on Metal

Stenciling metal surfaces is one of the best-known outlets for stencil art. Traditional American folk art is full of trays, kettles, canisters, and pitchers that have been stenciled. You may already own a lamp, watering can, or tray that is a prime candidate for stenciling. If you do not already own some metal piece, they are usually very easy to come by. Many hobby stores carry a line of unpainted metal planters, vases, and trays that are just perfect. We find that the Lee Ward's Company, which has retail stores across the country as well as a national mail-order craft business, is an excellent source. Remember too that outdoor mailboxes make great stencil subjects. With the new suburban craze for distinctive mailboxes, you'll be a style-setter with a stenciled entry.

Prepare stencils for metal using the material of your choice. The metal surface should, of course, be free of rust, dirt, and grease. Paint in the stencils with acrylics, oils, or model paints. When dry, spray with a fixative or give it a couple of coats of shellac to protect the design against all the rain, sleet, and snow it will have to endure.

## Stenciling on Plaster Walls and Ceilings.

Stenciled walls and ceilings can be absolutely breathtaking. Many restoration villages such as Deerfield, Massachusetts, and homes such as Boscobel Mansion, Garrison, New York, feature some very beautiful stencil work just as it was done in Colonial America.

Walls and ceilings should not provide any problems for the modern stenciler. Prepare them for stenciling as you would for regular painting. Make sure that the area is fairly smooth and clean. Stenciling will camouflage many of the minor bumps and cracks, but do try to eliminate major imperfections by using spackling compound or replastering wherever necessary. Remember that plaster is porous and tends to drink up paint. Its thirst also seems to increase with age. Before painting on a base coat, test a small area. If you find that too much paint is being absorbed, give the entire wall or ceiling a primer coat. This will seal the surface and it will be easy to apply the base coat and subsequent stencils.

As for the stencils, we recommend that you use acetate only as a stencil material. You will probably be repeating the same design over and over again and you will appreciate the durability and ease of working with acetate.

You can use either latex or oil-based paints for both the base coat and the stencil design.

*Here a stenciled wall border complements the four poster's stenciled quilt.*

Remember that if you are using latex paint, tint the base coat with acrylics and you will be assured of having perfectly blended colors.

Once the wall is stenciled, there is no further care or special treatment necessary.

## Stenciling on Baskets

You can achieve some nice results by stenciling on baskets. The essential thing here is making the right choice of a basket to work on. Those woven with wide strips are best as they provide a bit more leeway as far as placing a design and coloring it in on a fairly flat area. Think about decorating a large size bushel basket to hold magazines or put near a fireplace and fill it with wood. If you don't use a basket woven with wide strips, choose one that is very tightly woven with an almost flat texture to its surface. If you use a basket that is in-between the two types, you will run the risk of losing the design amid all the lumps and bumps of the basket's woven surface. The natural texture of the basket can also interfere with the placement and coloring-in of the stencil and you may end up with nothing more than a blob. If you have a basket that you are uncertain of, try stenciling it in some unobtrusive spot on the inside or bottom. If it doesn't work, at least you won't have ruined a good basket.

Use the stencil material of your choice. You can paint the basket itself before stenciling, although we prefer to leave a basket in its natural state. As for coloring-in, we find that marking pens work beautifully. If there is any problem with the design edges bleeding, try making just the outline of the stencil, then remove it and fill in with the rest of the color. If you don't care to use marking pens, try acrylics. Any other coloring agent will be much too much trouble.

Whatever coloring you use, coat the finished piece with shellac to preserve and protect the design. The colors can tend to fade through handling if they are not protected.

Remember too, that you can treat matchstick shades and bamboo curtains in the same manner as you would a basket.

## Stenciling Glass and Mirrors

Everyone under forty years of age must remember stenciling windows at holiday times. In Northport, New York, where we grew up, there was an annual window decorating contest at Halloween. Local merchants gave up their windows for a week or so to ghosts, witches, goblins, black cats and skeletons, full moons and pumpkins. Some of the "artists" worked freehand, but those of us who were less gifted used stencils for all or part of our windows. At Christmastime the storm windows and doors of private homes were decorated with snowmen, wreaths, trees, snowflakes, angels, Santas, and elves. As kids, we can remember tinting a pink liquid window cleaner and stenciling our designs on windows with it, following the directions that were advertised on T.V.

You can still decorate glass surfaces, only be a little more sophisticated about it. For seasonal greetings or designs that you have no wish to make permanent, cut out a design from the stencil material of your choice, and color it in with school paint. For more permanent designs, use enamels, acrylics, or oils. One woman we know has a city apartment that faces a brick wall less than three feet away. She turned the eyesore into a fantasy landscape by stenciling her windows with outsized morning glories, fluffy clouds, tiny houses, and rolling hills in bright colors. Another friend, this one a country resident, decorated her playroom windows with a vining philodendron stenciled delicately around each window edge.

You can also put designs on glass shower and tub enclosures. If you do, be sure to use an oil-based paint. Anything water-soluble will be ruined by moisture. Do not use shellac or spray fixatives on glass surfaces; it can make removal extremely difficult. Just let the design dry thoroughly and maintain the glass and the design with soap and water.

You can also try dressing up a medicine cabinet, vanity, or full-length mirror with stencils. Make sure that the mirrored surface is clean and dust-free. Cut stencils from the material of your choice. For coloring-in, use only oils, acrylics, or enamels.

You can apply stencils to glass pitchers, vases, glasses, and bowls. Use any stencil material you like. Use only enamels or oils, and make sure that the piece dries completely before using it.

## Stenciling Clay Pottery and Bricks

You can adorn the simple clay pots that house your plants and create a lovely garden environment. Stencil flowers on a pot that houses a nonflowering plant, or stencil the name of the plant right on the pot. The latter is especially nice if you are growing a collection of herbs.

Make sure that the pot you use is either new or completely clean. Examine it carefully for chips and cracks. You want one that is perfect for stenciling. Prepare a stencil from whatever material is most convenient. For coloring-in, we like to use marking pens. If you use them, keep in mind that the red clay does distort colors. Darker tones will hold up quite well, but lighter ones can be a problem and may not show up at all. Make a mark with the colors you like on the inside or on the bottom of the pot for testing. If you don't choose to color with marking pens, you can always use acrylics or enamels.

Some people like the shiny finish that a few coats of shellac provides. We have found from experience that if you coat the inside or outside of the pot, there is some difficulty in keeping plants healthy and growing. We would suggest not planting directly in the clay pot if you have sealed it with a finish of any kind. Just place a plant already in a smaller pot into the one you have stenciled to ensure that you won't lose a plant.

In addition to clay pots, you can stencil on bricks using the same procedure. A brick stenciled all over in a small pattern and coated with shellac makes an excellent doorstop. Or perhaps one of your rooms has an exposed brick wall or a brick fireplace. Even outdoor brickwork can be stenciled. If you stencil on fireplaces or outdoors, we don't suggest using marking pens, although you could use them on a brick wall inside of the house. Be sure to coat all stenciled brick surfaces with shellac after painting.

## Stenciling on Enamel and Porcelain

Highly glazed surfaces such as kitchen and bathroom tiles, refrigerators, even automobiles can all be stenciled.

In each case, prepare a stencil from the material of your choice. We are partial to acetate for any large areas that will contain repeat patterns.

For coloring-in on tiles that will be exposed to water, use model paints or a high-gloss enamel. There is also an excellent paint made for such surfaces by Epoxy which you can also use. For tiles that won't be effected by water, you can use artists enamels or acrylics. Model paints may be used on refrigerators and cars. Protect whatever surface you have stenciled with shellac.

## Stenciling on Linoleum

You can change the face of a plainly-tiled kitchen by stenciling right on the tiles. You can either make use of the tiles as separate entities or create a design that ignores them entirely as separate units.

Make sure to cut stencils from acetate for work on linoleum. Use only enamel paint to color in the design. Note that you will probably want to cut a number of stencils to make your work go faster. After the tiles have dried completely, coat the floor with two layers of polyurethane to protect the design.

Keep in mind that you can also stencil on the self-adhesive floor tiles before placing them on the floor. You would proceed in the same manner as with regular inlaid tiles, but you may want to substitute spray enamel paint for regular enamel. Either will work if the tiles are not laid down. Do not coat with polyurethane though until you have placed the tiles down in the positions you want.

This beautiful stenciled floor is the highlight of the room. Note also the stenciled hutch and dining chairs. All three are quite different, yet complement each other nicely.

Here the same hutch in a different color and setting is a companion to the traditionally-patterned Early American desk and stool.

Pictured at left are some of the delightful things you can stencil on paper. A decorated gift box becomes a present in itself and you can make place cards, invitations, greeting cards, and even wrapping paper.

Here are two pretty ideas for personal stationery. The design in green has a romantic art nouveau look, while the one in maroon and blue has a more solid deco feeling.

Designer linen are growing ever more popular. You can have an original of your own design by stenciling with acrylics on solid color sheets as we have done here.

Set a party table on a gaily-stenciled cloth with matching napkins. Note that the bread basket and cheese also feature stenciled designs.

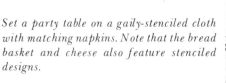

*Author Mary Jane Danley's son Matthew models a sweatshirt stenciled with a Guatemalan folk motif. The child's table and chair belonged to the authors as children and have been given a new life with bright paint and stencils.*

*Usually overlooked, stair risers can also be beautifully decorative when painted and stenciled.*

*Stenciling on cloth produced this bit of Victoriana. The stenciled design can also be filled in with crewel embroidery for those who are needlework enthusiasts.*

An early American farmhouse parlor featuring stenciled walls is on view at Old Sturbridge Village in Massachusetts.

Deerfield, Massachusetts is one of the East Coast's beautifully restored colonial villages. Careful attention to all original detail, of course included bringing wall stencils back to their original beauty. Shown here is the Hall Tavern Ballroom.

## Stenciling on Formica

Formica has long been a standby for sink counters and kitchen work areas. More recently it has grown popular as a finish on modern-design furniture: parson's tables, captain's beds, campaign furniture. It is an excellent smooth surface on which to stencil. New tables, cabinets, and headboards can be beautifully enhanced and old, scratched and otherwise pitted and marred pieces can be given a new lease on life.

You can cut stencils from either acetate or stencil paper for work on formica. The surface will need to be sanded to remove some of its glossiness. You may take your pick of base coats, although we do prefer to use latex paints. Acrylics or japan paints may be used for the actual stencil designs.

Whenever you stencil on formica, it is best to give the finished product several coats of polyurethane.

In this *How To* section are instructions for rejuvenating a very old and pitted sink counter and splashboard. The idea only occurred to us after an investigation into the cost of replacing it. The price of a brand-new counter was prohibitively high and an alternative solution became necessary.

## HOW-TO

# Other Surfaces

Now you are prepared to stencil on just about any natural or man-made surface that you can think of. We have included projects for formica, red clay pots, plaster walls, and a basket. Have fun with these and continue to enjoy stenciling on your own.

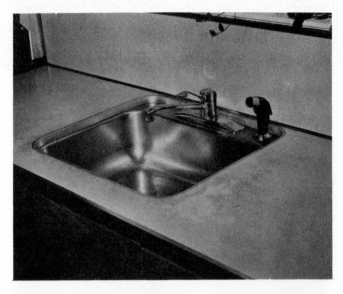

*The price of replacing this worn-out sink counter was so outrageous that we were determined to take the matter into our own hands.*

*First we gave the counter a light sanding and then a thorough scrubbing. Next we taped all the edges with masking tape for nice clean edges. And then a coat of Flash-Bond which gave us this smooth and even surface to work on.*

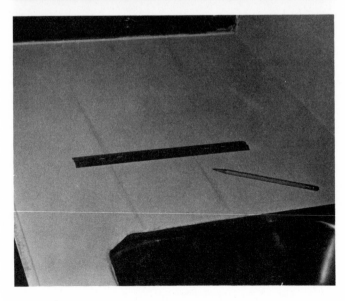

*After the Flash-Bond dried, a grid was sketched right onto the counter in pencil (you can also use chalk). Each square would eventually incorporate a tile.*

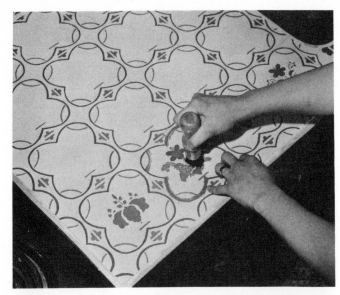

First all of the borders were painted in.
Once they dried, it was time to apply the
central motifs.

Note that when you are working stencils to
duplicate hand-painted tiles, it is essential to
align the lines that will eventually depict
grouting, but it becomes more authentic
looking if you do not line up the designs
exactly. Hand-painted tiles rarely match
exactly and this is indeed part of their
charm. Try to incorporate such deliberate
imperfections in your tile designs as we did
here.

Here is the finished counter, painted and
coated with polyurethane. We opted to do
only every other tile on the splashboard to
prevent the piece from looking too
cluttered.

# FORMICA COUNTER TOP AND SPLASHBOARD

## Materials:

sandpaper

strong detergent

Flash Bond #400W white Primer and Sealer

flat white latex paint

Grumbacher acrylic paint in yellow ochre light

chalk

acetate

tracing paper

glass

masking tape

Grifhold No. 113 knife

japan paints in raw sienna and white

small stencil brushes (Nos. 00–1)

Eberhard Faber fine point marking pen in dark putty

polyurethane

brushes for applying primer and sealer, base coat, and polyurethane

1. Sand to degloss and even the surface. Wash with detergent and allow to dry thoroughly.

2. Apply two coats of primer and sealer allowing the counter to dry thoroughly between applications. (*Note:* The counter we stenciled was a medium yellow, a darker counter might require more Flash Bond.)

3. Mix the flat white latex and yellow ochre light in a ration of two to one for the base coat. (We color matched it to the linoleum floor of the kitchen.) Paint base coat and allow to dry thoroughly, applying a second coat at that time if necessary.

4. Trace designs from the Design Portfolio. Cut an acetate stencil for each following the instructions given in Chapter Two.

5. Using chalk, mark off "grouting" lines on both counter top and splashboard. Make sure that the lines meet at the juncture of the two as they would if you were cementing in actual tiles.

6. Create three shades of brown with the japan paints and color in the designs, making sure to clean stencils thoroughly between applications.

7. When stencil designs are dry, apply polyurethane to counter and splashboard. Because of the constant heavy use the area receives, we gave four coats and recommend that you do the same.

*This border design is painted on a plaster wall that was prepared according to the general instructions given here, using latex paint as a base for the stencil design.*

## STENCILED WALL (with window(s) in center)

Materials:

latex wall paint in a medium dusty rose, or other solid color of your choice

acetate

tracing paper

glass

masking tape

Grifhold No. 113 knife

latex paint in the palest shade of rose

small stencil brushes (Nos. 00–1)

1. Prepare and paint wall following the previous general instructions.
2. Trace design from the Design Portfolio.
3. Cut an acetate stencil following the instructions given in Chapter Two.
4. Use masking tape to secure the stencil to the wall. Follow the illustration as a guide for routing the work around the window. When painting, be sure to clean the stencil thoroughly between applications.

*Divide the design at the dotted line to make the top right and left corners. Fill in in between with the regular scalloped design, adding or subtracting scallops to fit the window.*

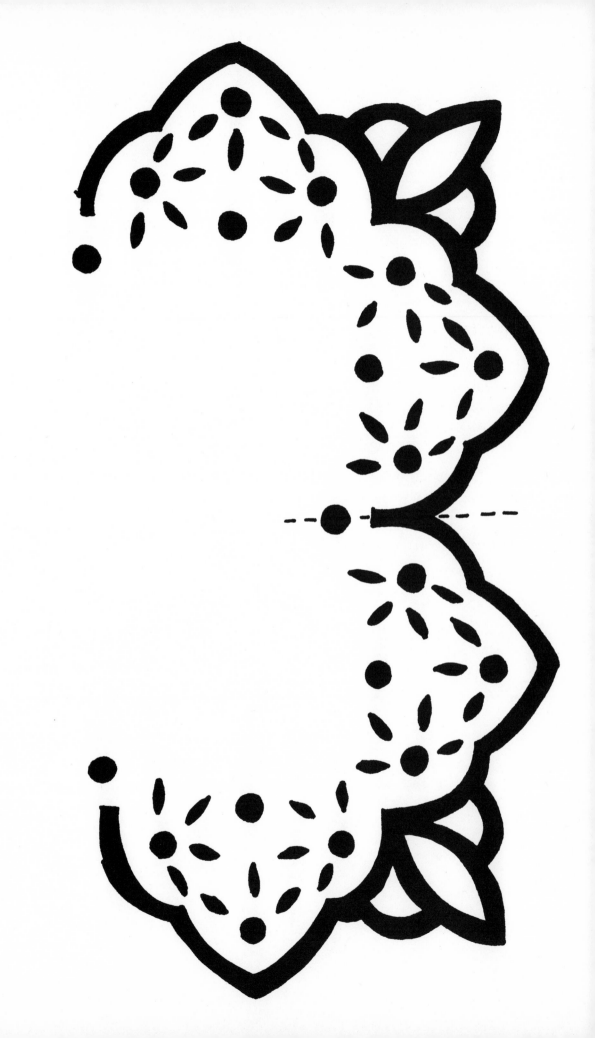

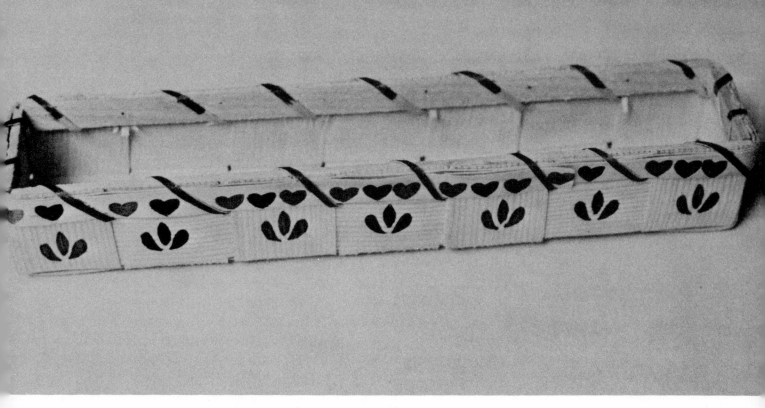

*Felt-tip markers were the coloring agents used on this broad-woven basket. Note that broad, flat pieces such as those used here or on fruit and bushel baskets are most easily stenciled.*

## BASKET

Materials:

tracing paper

oak tag or manila paper

X-acto knife

cardboard

masking tape

Eberhard Faber fine point marking pens in bright red and black

shellac and brush (optional)

1. Trace designs from the Design Portfolio and transfer to oak tag following the instructions given in Chapter Two.
2. Cut the stencil using the X-acto knife. Make one strip of three or four same sized hearts and another of two of the other motif (one for reds and one for blacks).
3. Color in, holding the stencil down with the fingers of one hand and applying color with the other. Alternate red and black as you go along and around the basket.
4. If desired, finish the basket with one or two coats of clear shellac.

# CLAY FLOWER POTS

## Materials:

acetate

tracing paper

glass

masking tape

Grifhold No. 113 knife

2 clay flower pots and plates, either new or very clean and dry (no dirt should be clinging anywhere)

Eberhard Faber fine point marking pens in magenta and turquoise

shellac and brush (optional)


1. Trace designs from the Design Portfolio.
2. Cut acetate stencils following instructions given in Chapter Two.
3. Secure stencil to the pot with masking tape. Color in the bottom of the pot first and then the rim. (*Note:* The marking pens are actually transparent color and the effect on the pot will not be as vivid as on paper.) Note also that the polka-dotted dish was done without a stencil, the dots were applied at random around the edge.
5. Coat with shellac if desired, but take care not to plant directly in the pot if you do (see previous general instructions).

*Let flowers bloom and plants grow in stenciled clay pots. These whimsical pots were colored in with felt-tip marking pens.*

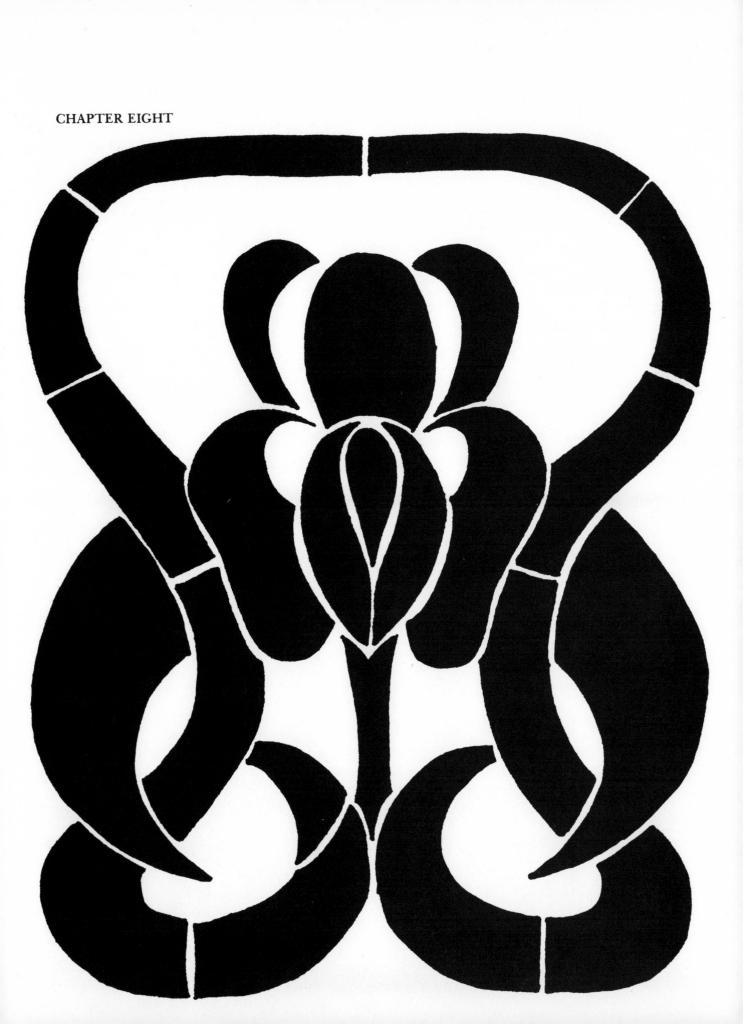

# CHAPTER EIGHT

# Design Portfolio

WE ARE PRESENTING for your stenciling pleasure a collection of designs most of which were created especially for this book by Mary Jane Danley and have never appeared anywhere else.

These exclusive designs cover a broad range of choices from flowers, fruits, vegetables, and birds to primitive art to the most whimsical and charming creatures that you could wish for to decorate children's furniture and clothing. Included also are border designs and an alphabet.

Let us also note that in addition to the designs that you will find here in the portfolio, other usable designs appear throughout the book. Each chapter, for instance, opens with a wonderful full-page pattern. Also designs shown for practice cutting should not be neglected as potential stencils. Border designs appear with general information about handling corners. You'll come up with a few other little surprise designs here and there as you browse through the book. It is all meant to be used and we certainly hope that you will take advantage of all that is here.

You should have great fun sorting through and deciding which ones to use and how you will use them. We made an effort to repeat designs earlier in the book so that you could see how a single design can appear quite different in looks simply by changing its color or using it with another design or by using it for a different purpose.

You can use any of these designs alone or try them in groups to create a larger picture. Enlarge or reduce them as you see fit.

As far as using the designs, keep in mind when tracing that the black areas are those which are meant to be cut out. In most cases, a design is in solid black. You may want to break the basic design down into two or three stencils if you want to use them in a lot of colors. We are leaving this decision to you. You will note also that some of the designs do show a second stencil done in dotted lines. This is because you would not be able to complete the design even in a single color without cutting a second stencil.

Finally, the most important advice of all—enjoy yourself as you stencil from start—with choosing a design—to finish.

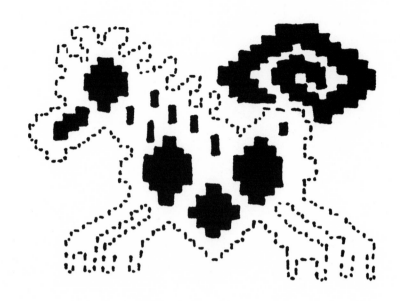

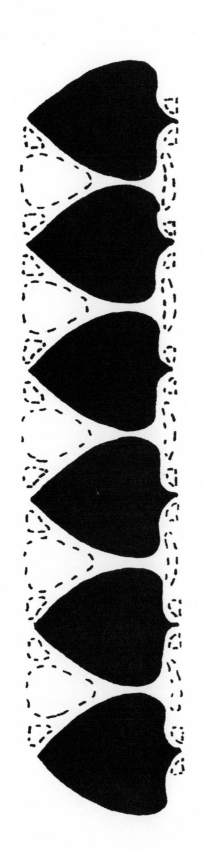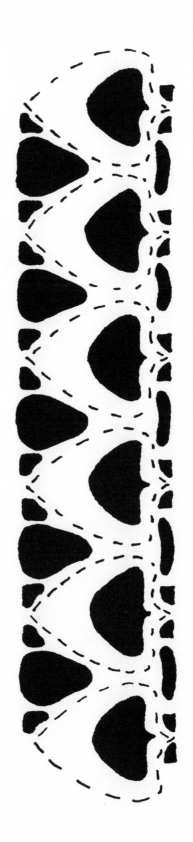

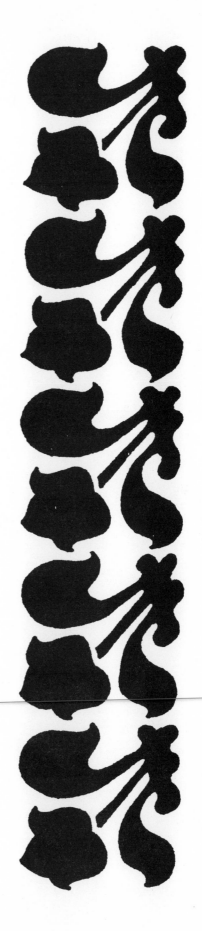

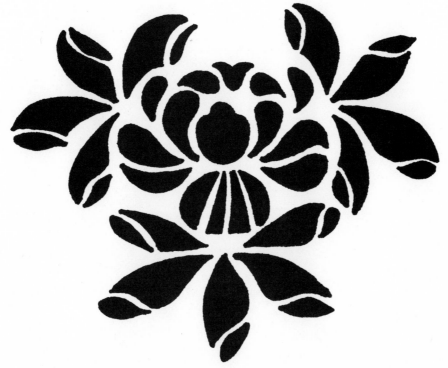

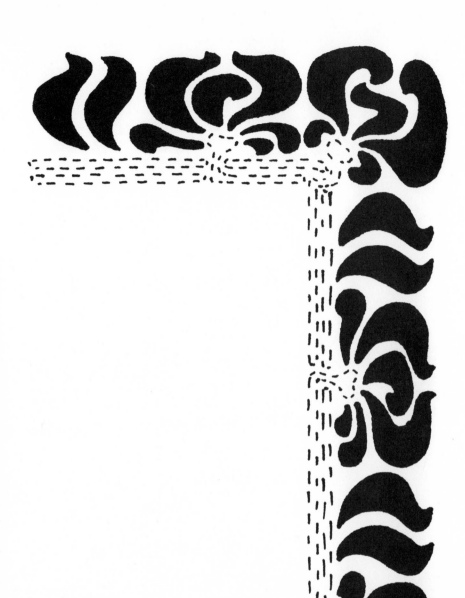
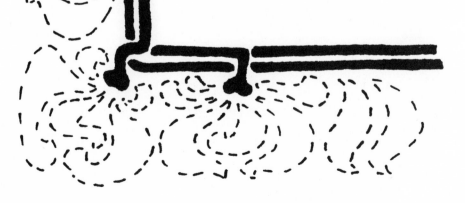

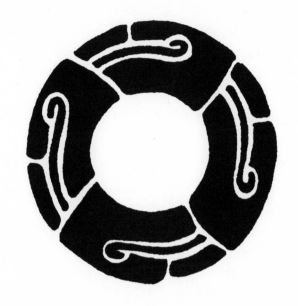

A.

To create this circular design, cut out the stencils as shown, matching them at the dotted lines.

**B.**

*Match up the two halves of the circle by lining up the dotted lines.*

# Bibliography

The following books have proved invaluable to us as sources of designs and design inspirations. We would like to share them with you. If you are interested in stenciling, you will certainly want some or all of them in your own collection. In addition, they are useful in almost all other crafts.

Chapman, Suzanne E. *Early American Design Motifs*. New York: Dover Publications, Inc., 1974.

Encisco, Jorge. *Designs from Pre-Columbian Mexico*. New York: Dover Publications, Inc., 1971.

Hawley, W.M. *Chinese Folk Designs*, New York: Dover Publications, Inc., 1949.

Hornung, Clarence. *Allover Patterns for Designers and Craftsmen*. New York: Dover Books, Inc., 1975.

Humbert, Claude. *Ornamental Design: A source book with 1000 Illustrations*. New York: A Studio Book, The Viking Press, 1970.

Lipman, Jean. *Techniques in American Folk Decoration*, New York: Dover Publications, Inc., 1951.

Loeb, Marcia. *Art Deco Designs and Motifs*. New York: Dover Publications, Inc., 1972.

The Matsuya Piece-Goods Store. *Japanese Design Motifs*. New York: Dover Publications, Inc., 1972

Menten, Theodore *Art Nouveau & Early Art Deco Type and Design*. New York: Dover Publications, Inc., 1972.

Mirow, Gregory *A Treasury of Design for Artsists and Craftsmen*. New York: Dover Publications, Inc., 1969.

Seguy, E.A. *Full-Color Floral Designs in the Art Nouveau Style*. New York: Dover Publications, Inc., 1977.

Sibbett, Ed, Jr. *Stained Glass Pattern Book*, New York: Dover Publications, Inc., 1976.

Waring, Janet *Early American Stencils on Walls and Furniture*, New York: Dover Publications, Inc., 1968.

Williams, Geoffrey *African Designs from Traditional Sources*, New York: Dover Publications, Inc., 1971.

Wilson, Nadine *A Guide to Decoration in The Early American Manner*, Rutland, Vermont and Tokyo, Japan: Charles E. Tuttle Company, 1965.

# Supply Sources

IF YOU ARE among the very lucky, you will be able to find everything you need at a local art shop or paint store. Often, however you will find that some vital blade for cutting or tube of paint eludes your most diligent efforts. For those times, we have included here a list of suppliers. It has been our experience that the retail stores will fill an order by mail as long as you prepay for the purchase and postage.

## Retail Stores

Arthur Brown and Bro., Inc.
2 West 46th Street
New York, NY 10036

Janovic Plaza
1292 First Avenue
New York, NY 10021

Pearl Paint Co., Inc.
2411 Hempstead Turnpike
East Meadow, NY

308 Canal Street
New York, NY

803 Route 17
Paramus, NJ

1033 East Oakland Park Boulevard
Ft. Lauderdale, FL
  *Note:* We love Pearl Paint. We have found them to be consistently helpful and always in possession of a full stock of knives, acetate, stencil paper of all weights, acrylics, gesso, japan paint, and the finest and fullest selection of stencil brushes anywhere.

Lee Ward's
Elgin, IL 60120
  Write to the company for the location of the retail store nearest you.

## Mail Order Suppliers

Herrschners, Inc.
Hoover Road
Stevens Point, WI 54481

Lee Ward's
Elgin, IL 60120

Merribee
Box 9680
Fort Worth, TX 76107

The Guildcraft Co. of Buffalo
3158 Main Street
Dept. 177-AH
Buffalo, NY 14214

Earth Guild/Grateful Union
Mail Order Service
15 North Tudor Street
Cambridge, MA 02139

Craft Supplies Supermarket
Oliver Press
1400 Ryan Creek Road
Willits, CA 95490

## Miscellaneous

Wilton Enterprises
833 West 115th Street
Chicago, IL 60643
  For food stenciling supplies write for their catalog.

Cohasset Colonials by Hagerty
16 Ship Street
Cohasset, MA 02025
  For furniture kits, write for their catalog.

Yield House
North Conway, NH
  For furniture kits, paints, and antiquing supplies, write for their catalog.